D0560783

Chocolate Principles to Live By

Theresa Cheung

MJF BOOKS
NEW YORK

Published by MJF Books
Fine Communications
322 Eighth Avenue
New York, NY 10001

Chocolate Principles to Live By
LC Control Number 2005936866
ISBN-13: 978-1-56731-756-5
ISBN-10: 1-56731-756-1

Originally published by Conari Press, an imprint of Red Wheel/Weiser LLC, under the title *Better Than Sex*. This special edition is published by MJF Books in arrangement with Conari Press, an imprint of Red Wheel/Weiser LLC.

Book design by Maxine Ressler

Printed in the United States of America.

MJF Books and the MJF colophon are trademarks of Fine Creative Media, Inc.

VB   10   9   8   7   6   5   4   3   2   1

*This book is dedicated to the fifteen
out of every ten individuals who our research
tells us love chocolate!*

Contents

Acknowledgments ix

Introduction: **Chocolate Magic** 1

Chocolate Principles to Live By 5

1. **Discover the Sweet Center** 7

2. **Let It Melt in Your Mouth** 31

3. **Chocolate Makes You Feel Good** 57

4. **No Need to Eat the Whole Box** 75

5. **A Little Good Chocolate Goes a Long Way** 91

6. **Pass the Chocolates** 111

7. **Chocolate Heaven** 133

Afterword: **Chocolate 'Round the World** 157

Appendix: **Guilt-Free Indulgence** 163

Acknowledgments

Thank you to Jan and everyone at Red Wheel/Weiser/Conari for allowing me to combine two of my passions—chocolate and writing. Thank you to Ray and our two beautiful children, Robert and Ruth, for helping me eat my way through all the research. And thanks to Dr. Priscilla Stuckey for her fine editing.

Chocolate Magic

Silky, smooth, sensuous, sweet, rich, intense, creamy, seductive—and deliriously delicious. Small wonder that chocolate is a consuming passion the world over. But given chocolate's sinful image, guilt often goes hand in hand with enjoying this indulgent treat. However, there is good news about the darker side of chocolate. Recent studies prove what we chocoholics have known all along: Chocolate doesn't cause all the problems it's accused of, like acne, obesity, and addiction. In fact, eaten sensibly, chocolate can protect your heart, boost your mood, and even help you live longer. Yes, chocolate can be good for you!

It was after one of those only-chocolate-will-do, now-I-feel-good-ahh moments that I began to think about my love affair with chocolate and how it never fails to lift me up. What if I could devour life with the same commitment and passion? Some spend a lifetime searching for enlightenment. Others find it in the here and now. Chocolate is the food of the gods: energy, comfort, and oneness all wrapped up together. In an unreliable world, I know I can always count on it to lift me up. What could I learn from this? What links could I find between chocolate, creativity, and spirituality?

That's what prompted me to write a book that relates the principles of a contented life to the melt-in-the-mouth irresistible enjoyment of chocolate. The seven principles of chocolate wisdom are as uplifting, comforting, and as pleasurable as the food they celebrate. They offer a guide for you to enjoy your life through chocolate—without feeling guilty.

You can read this book from beginning to end, or you can dip into it for daily inspiration. As you read, why not surrender to your craving and melt a little piece of heaven in your mouth? Chocolate tastes like paradise—and it's something we all deserve from time to time.

Bite-Sized Chocolate Facts

Seven billion pounds of chocolate are manufactured each year in the United States. Statistics show that the average person in the United States eats about 12 pounds of chocolate each year!

Chocolate is America's favorite flavor. A survey of 1,000 American adults found chocolate was ranked as their favorite flavor for dessert and sweet snacks by 3 to 1.

In the United Kingdom the average consumption of chocolate per person is 16 pounds per year. However, the world's top consumers of chocolate are the Swiss, closely followed by the Norwegians, then the Belgians, Dutch, and Germans.

Chocolate manufacturers currently use 40 percent of the world's almonds and 20 percent of the world's peanuts. American chocolate manufacturers use about 1.5 billion pounds of milk a year; only the cheese and ice cream industries use more.

All United States and Russian space missions have included chocolate rations for nutrition and morale. In World War II, chocolate was given to millions of troops.

Chocolate first appeared on film when Jean Harlow ate it in 1933's *Dinner at Eight*. Chocolate syrup was used as blood in the chilling shower scene from Alfred Hitchcock's *Psycho*.

Chocolate may well be a crucial ingredient in the fight to save the world's rainforests. Because chocolate comes from cacao trees, which thrive in the rainforest environment, it makes sense for the future of chocolate to preserve a system of agriculture that has been around for thousands of years.

Chocolate has a long shelf life—up to 18 months.

The melting point of cocoa butter is just below normal body temperature, which is why chocolate melts in your mouth.

Chocolate is the food we crave the most. Forty percent of women and 15 percent of men crave it, according to researchers reporting in the *Journal of the American Diabetic Association*.

According to Cadbury's spokesman, Tony Bilsborough, a massive 60 percent of women would rather have a one-to-one with a chocolate bar than have sex!

Chocolate Principles to Live By

1. **Discover the Sweet Center:** Positive change takes place from the inside out.
2. **Let It Melt in Your Mouth**: Make your life extraordinary.
3. **Chocolate Makes You Feel Good**: Stop feeling guilty.
4. **No Need to Eat the Whole Box**: Have the strength to say yes to what is important and no to what isn't.
5. **A Little Good Chocolate Goes a Long Way**: Expect nothing less than the best.
6. **Pass the Chocolates**: Give and receive in equal measure.
7. **Chocolate Heaven**: You can heal your life.

Discover the Sweet Center

ABOUT CHOCOLATE: Choose your favorite filled chocolate or truffle. Let the chocolate sit in your mouth for a few seconds to release its wonderful flavors and aromas. Then, chew slowly to discover the center. Take your time, and allow the union of chocolate and center to melt slowly in your mouth. Delicious!

ABOUT LIFE: Positive change takes place from the inside out.

*O*pen a box of assorted chocolates, and you see before you a microcosm of life. There is pleasure to be found, but you may have to experiment until you find it. (Why else would they include centers like pineapple cream or lime nougat?) It's much more satisfying when you know what's inside before you make a choice. It's much the same in life. If you want to lead a happy, contented life, you need to know what's going on inside you. You need to know what you like and what you don't like.

Finding Out What's Inside

If you don't know what makes you feel good, how can you make positive changes? The first chocolate principle is about discovering your center, getting to know yourself better. And the way to do this is by developing your self-awareness. This means looking deep within at the way you think and feel about yourself and your life.

Are you happy with your life? What is important to you? What makes you feel sad? What makes you feel good?

Don't worry if you don't know the answers to these questions. The important thing is that you start asking them and get into the habit of reflecting on why you think and feel the way you do. Each time you pause a moment to notice yourself doing the things you do or wonder why you feel the way you do, you will be getting to know yourself a little better, and this is the first step on the road toward a happier life. Self-knowledge is, after all, the beginning of wisdom

Do You Dare Discover Your Center?

The center or filling that you love can tell you a lot about yourself. What is it about the center that attracts you? These centers—their smell, their taste, their texture—link into your moods, your thoughts, your self-esteem. By understanding what the centers suggest, you may be able to understand your feelings better. So why not take some time out with chocolate and find your center?

Almond: Quick thinking and freedom loving, you thrive on change and variety. You can also appear flippant at times, and you may have a tendency to flit from one thing or person to another.

Apricot: Gentle and self-assured, you like to help others and create warmth and security in your surroundings. You can also lack patience and find it hard to trust others.

Brazil nut: Your life appears perfect, and you like to be seen at all the right places. But sometimes despite outward appearances, you feel vulnerable and anxious on the inside.

Caramel, hard: People can rely on you, and you like to get things done. Routine is important to you. The downside is that you may find it hard to listen to and respect the points of view of others.

Caramel, soft: You are comfortable and easygoing—too easygoing sometimes, and you don't get the credit or the reward you deserve.

Caramel with nuts: You are everyone's friend. You have charisma but can also be a bit of a temptress or tease.

Cherry: You have a lust for life and love. Your energy is incredible. Just watching you makes others feel tired.

Chocolate: You can laugh at yourself and don't take yourself too seriously. You enjoy the game of life and look to the future with healthy optimism.

Coconut: Creative and artistic, you feel drawn to music, dance, and the rhythm of life, but you might appear a bit flighty to others.

Coffee: A deep thinker who enjoys the art of conversation and debate, you have an open mind. You may have a tendency to be impatient or to stay so busy and focused on work that you forget to attend to loved ones.

Fudge: You have a relaxed, graceful approach to life, but it's important to you to make your mark on the world. When you can't achieve what you want, you feel stuck and frustrated.

Ginger: Success and power are important for you, and you are prepared to work for them—even if that means going it alone and making sacrifices.

Hazelnut: You are a nature lover and rely heavily on your intuition, which often brings you great success. You may have to fight against shyness.

Honeycomb crunch: You are full of great ideas and creative energy. For you, the journey is more important than the destination, which means that you may begin projects and not see them through to the end.

Lemon: You like to do your own thing and are not worried about what other people think. Sometimes you can be a little self-absorbed and need to lighten up.

Lime: You have a good sense of direction in your life, and you listen to your feelings. Having space or alone time is important to you to gather strength, because you can be easily hurt or offended.

Marshmallow: You are very sociable and like to party and have people around you. The danger is that you can get bored quickly.

Mint: Cool and sophisticated, you have bags of charisma. It's not that you don't want to commit, it's just that life is too exciting and you love your freedom.

Orange: You need to find meaning in life, to discover yourself and fulfill your spiritual needs. Don't forget that you have physical and emotional needs, too.

Peanut: You are an outdoor kind of person. Time is precious to you, and you fit a lot—sometimes too much—into your day.

Pecan: Staying young in body and mind is important to you, and this makes you an appealing and fun-loving person.

Pineapple: You have a strong sense of fun and adventure. You enjoy learning and love talking—sometimes too much.

Raisin: Health-conscious and disciplined, you respect yourself and those around you. Sometimes, though, you are a little too hard on yourself.

Raspberry: You like life to be fun and simple and when it gets complicated, you can feel naive and lost.

Strawberry: A loving and thoughtful person, you are an eternal optimist with lots of love to give. Your generosity means that you are often taken advantage of.

Turkish delight: Spirituality is central to your life, and you are always looking for more in life than the material. The danger occurs when, in trying to seek meaning, you lose touch with reality.

Walnut: You have a fresh, problem-solving approach to life. Although a good communicator, you may prefer your own company.

Of course, this is just a fun exercise. Walnut-center lovers are not all artistic, and strawberry-center lovers are not all loving and caring. But playing the game can help get you thinking along the right lines. What kind of person are you? What do you like about yourself? What are your strengths? What are your weaknesses? What is really going on inside you?

Take a Good Long Look at Yourself

Take a good long look at the way you lead your life. What things drag you down? What things, apart from chocolate, lift you up?

It might help to act as an observer on your own life. Step outside yourself for a moment and just observe what you think, feel, say, and do. Observing yourself is a well-known technique for improving self-awareness. Watching yourself can help you separate what you think and feel from who you are. You will see that throughout your day, thoughts and feelings constantly flow through you. You will see that as powerful as these feelings and thoughts are, they are separate from you. You are the one who allows yourself to experience them. You are the one in charge.

As you get to know yourself better, you will start to recognize events, patterns of behavior, responses, or attitudes that make you unhappy. Perhaps your job is making you feel stressed or your relationship isn't as fulfilling as it could be or you are doing things because you feel pressured by friends and family, or perhaps you just feel low and don't know why. Whatever the reason, once you are able to identify and acknowledge that you aren't as happy as you could be, you can start thinking about ways to make positive changes. You can only change what you acknowledge.

All Change Starts with You

But how do you begin making changes? Simple. You begin with YOU.

Once you have recognized the need to make a positive

change, the place to begin is with yourself—not your partner, your children, your family, your friends, your wardrobe, your weight, or your work. Everything starts with you. Positive change always begins on the inside.

You can immediately begin to feel happier about yourself and your life by changing the way you feel about yourself. When you feel good about yourself, you feel calm, confident, and in control. When you don't feel good about yourself, everything starts to go wrong. Getting chocolate with an unpleasant-tasting center is a big disappointment for a chocoholic. Don't let that happen in your life too. That's why changing from the inside out—making sure that you feel good about yourself or have good self-esteem—is the first chocolate principle to master.

Do You Feel Good about Yourself?

To find out, you need to ask yourself certain questions:

* ❀ Do I like myself?
* ❀ Do I think I'm a good human being?
* ❀ Do I deserve to be loved?
* ❀ Do I deserve to be happy?
* ❀ Do I really feel that I'm an okay person?

If you find it hard to answer yes to all the questions, then negative feelings about yourself are limiting your chances of happiness. Furthermore, you are probably giving out signals that you don't really love, like, and value yourself, which makes it harder for other people to love, like, and value you too.

Feeling Good on the Inside

Feeling good about yourself is a lifelong goal. Don't expect it to happen overnight. Chocolate is one tried and trusted way to lift your spirits, but however wonderful and satisfying the chocolate boost is, it's still a short-term fix. Below you'll find more lasting ways to help you feel good on the inside. Try them and see what an immediate difference they make. Then, turn to Principle #2 to see how you can transform this new awareness into positive change.

Let Yourself Off the Hook

Forgive yourself when you mess up. Let yourself off the hook. Taking out the whips and beating yourself up for the things that went wrong will do little to improve the way you feel about yourself. It's like kicking a horse that can't keep up. The horse is going to start thinking, "Why should I bother going anywhere? I can't go as fast as you want me to, so I may as well sit down and not move at all."

When things go wrong and you do something really stupid, be kinder to yourself. Watch the way you speak to yourself. Don't put yourself down, but instead speak to yourself gently—as if you were a small child with an opportunity to learn something. Use respectful self-talk instead of berating yourself. Shift your tone and choice of words. Use neutral words instead of charged negative ones. For example, "that's too bad" instead of "that's horrible," "didn't work this time" instead of "complete failure," and so on. Take a deep breath and calm down before launching into action or self-criticism.

Each time things don't go according to plan, remind yourself that it could always be worse. For example, you've lost a job—but you haven't lost your skills or your experience. You've gained ten unwanted pounds—but you haven't gained even more. You ate two more chocolate bars than you should have—but you didn't eat three. This will help swing your mind back to a more hopeful place, recognizing that you do have strengths. From that awareness, focus on how you can put them to work more effectively.

Don't forget that "to err is human," and most of us learn by getting things wrong before we get them right. So stop beating yourself up. Blaming yourself or others for things that went wrong in your life won't accomplish anything and will only make you feel powerless. The past is just that—the past. Learn what went wrong and why. Make amends if you need to, focus on what you did that was positive, and move on. You can't change what you did in the past. Let it go. "One of the keys to happiness," said writer Rita Mae Brown, "is a bad memory."

Remind yourself that you did the best that you could do, and now focus on the present moment. Accept responsibility, learn from your mistakes, and turn any regret you may have into resolve to make a positive difference from this day forward.

Use Your Intuition

> We understand each other, chocolate and I. My husband says I can hear chocolate.
>
> —Maria Heatter, cookbook author

If you want to find happiness you need to be true to yourself. You need to follow your instincts. This means working with your intuition. What do we mean by intuition? *Webster's Dictionary* defines it as gaining knowledge without reasoning or deduction. It's your gateway to a wisdom that is deeper and broader than your mind.

Intuition is being aware of something without being aware of how you know it. Intuition is our inner wisdom, and it plays a key role in our success. Some people are more intuitive than others, but there is growing evidence that we all possess this ability to some degree.

Wouldn't it be great if we could always rely on our intuition to guide us safely through life and stop us from making mistakes or taking wrong turns? Unfortunately, it doesn't work that way. Intuitive powers aren't always easy to read or summon at will. Intuition is mysterious and elusive, but one thing we do know: intuition tends to come to us when we are in a relaxed state of mind.

Ever remember thinking, "It's right on the tip of my tongue," but however hard you try you couldn't quite recall it? Then, you get on with your day, and later, seemingly from nowhere, the answer popped into your head. Intuition works in a similar way. Say that you are facing a problem, maybe at work or in your personal life. You have turned the matter over in your head, and when a solution won't present itself, you let go of it and stop thinking about it. You relax and turn your attention to something else. The problem slips into your subconscious mind, and your intuition gets to work scanning all the information you have stored and making connections. Then right out of the blue, an answer comes to you.

Intuition works better when you feel relaxed. The most favorable conditions for receiving intuitive messages are times of quiet and serenity, when your logical mind is subdued or shut down. If your life is busy and cluttered with constant to-dos, the distractions will be so loud that your intuition won't be able to make itself heard. Activities designed to calm the mind, such as meditation, yoga, or tai chi, might help, and you can do a lot of other things to encourage your intuition to bubble toward the surface.

Take some time for yourself away from distractions such as TV, radio, and noisy kids, and use the time to think, imagine, and dream. You may use this time to take a relaxing bath or walk or listen to music or stare out the window at the sky. The next time you enjoy your chocolate, just let your worries and fears melt away. Simply enjoy the delicious taste, and take that laid-back feeling with you into your daily routine. It doesn't matter what you do as long as you allow all directed thought to leave your mind and let your intuition take center stage. Then, when you least expect it, flashes of inspiration may come. Set aside time each day for a break of some kind, and this will make all the difference in connecting with your intuitive powers.

Your intuition may come to you clearly first thing in the morning, or it may come to you in a meaningful dream. Why not keep a notebook and record your dreams? Don't worry about books that interpret dreams; what matters is how YOU interpret the images. You may find that your body sends you a message from your intuition—a headache when you feel stressed, for example. Or things that have special meaning to you, such as a song or a food, may pop into your mind at a time when you need to feel supported, giving you peace of mind and courage. Your intuition may also speak to you in sections— a bit now, a bit later—and it is only when you have all the pieces of the puzzle that things become clear.

But how can you tell when your intuition is speaking? After all, our heads are always full of thoughts and voices telling us things.

When you know something intuitively, you just know it. There is a quiet and calm about it that is very different from the noisiness of fear. If the thoughts in your head are full of shame, fear, guilt, anxiety, and judgment, this isn't your intuition talking; your intuition tends to be warmer, gentler, kinder, and nonjudgmental. However, your intuition might tell you that something doesn't feel right or that this isn't right for you and it's time to move on or change direction and find something that works better. There may be no words at all, just a gut feeling that this isn't right for you.

If you want to lead a happy, fulfilled life, trust your instincts more. Let your intuition work for you. Get into the habit of carrying a pen and paper around or taking note of any thoughts that come to you randomly that sound like your intuition talking. They don't have to be earth-shattering, just simple thoughts you have as you go about your routine. At the end of the day, review what you have written, and see if a pattern emerges in the days and weeks that follow. Don't try to force the process. Instead, be patient and trust yourself to know what is best for you. Start listening to your hunches more, and see your life change for the better.

Smile More

How do you feel when you've had a really good laugh? You feel good all over—cleaned out and ready to start afresh. Laughing and smiling actually have great health benefits. They stimulate the production of endorphins (your body's natural painkillers), which produce a natural high. When you see the funny side of life, you are more able to put things in perspective; it's easier to ask yourself if your problem really does matter so much.

What incredible benefits! However fed up you feel, it surely is worth trying to find something to laugh about. If you put a smile on your face, people are more likely to smile back at you, and that will make you feel good. Seek out what makes you laugh—a book, a video, a friend, an activity. Go for laughter; it still is the best medicine. It's hard to feel bad about yourself and your life when you are having a really good laugh.

Chocolate Fun to Bring a Smile to Your Face

❖ I have this theory that chocolate slows down the aging process. It may not be true, but do I dare take the chance?

❖ To keep chocolate from melting, eat it faster.

❖ Chocolate-covered raisins, cherries, orange slices, and strawberries all count as fruit, so make sure you get enough.

❖ A balanced diet consists of items from the five major food groups: dairy, grains, meats, fruits and vegetables, and chocolate.

❖ Whoever said money couldn't buy happiness was only kidding. The best things go for $5.99 and up at the chocolate counter.

❖ Chocolate is cheaper than therapy, and you don't need an appointment.

❖ Man cannot live by chocolate alone — but woman can.

❖ It's not that chocolates are a substitute for love, love is a substitute for chocolate. Chocolate is — let's face it — far more reliable than a man.

❖ There is nothing better than a good friend — except a good friend with chocolate.

❖ Nine out of ten people like chocolate, and the tenth person always lies.

❖ Coffee, chocolate, men — some things are just better when they are rich.

❖ I'd give up chocolate, but I'm no quitter.

* Strength is the ability to break a piece of chocolate with your bare hands and then eat just one of the pieces.
* Put "eat chocolate" at the top of your to-do list today. That way you'll get at least one thing done.
* Chocolate is nature's way of making up for Mondays.
* Chocolate is an aphrodisiac; it increases the desire for more chocolate.
* I've never met a chocolate I didn't like.
* Chocolate makes everyone smile—even bankers.

Sweet Like Chocolate

When you feel low, one of the best tonics is to do something for someone else. Why? Because it's hard to feel bad about yourself when you're busy thinking of other people. Ironically, a by-product of helping others is feeling wonderful yourself.

So why not go out of your way to make everybody's life, including your own, a bit sweeter today? Say hello to someone who is lonely, hold the door open or give up your seat to someone else, volunteer for a good cause, pick up trash, wash the dirty dishes, be kind, or just smile. There are so many ways to make a positive difference in the lives of others and in the process feel better about yourself.

Center Your Life on Values

Now that you are beginning to discover more about yourself and to think about ways to feel good, let's get to the core of the matter and find out what is really inside you. Is your center rich and rewarding, or is it bland and disappointing?

Feeling rich from the inside out means centering your life not on people or things such as work, money, or appearance, but on deeply held values and principles. Centering your life on anything else but positive values is a recipe for disaster. If all you think about is work, then an upset is going to send you into meltdown. If all you think about is your partner, then your life won't be as fulfilling as it could be. If the opinions of your friends are all that matter to you, you will feel vulnerable when those friends move on or let you down. But if you base your life on your values, you will have the inner strength and resolve you need.

What are values? Values are things like honesty, respect, love, loyalty, generosity, humility, reliability, and responsibility. There are many more, and your heart will easily recognize them. To grasp why positive values matter so much, imagine your life based on the opposites. It's impossible to be happy through hate, deception, or anger.

Living according to your values and principles is not easy, especially if those around you aren't doing it. But as the saying goes, "My strength is the strength of ten because my heart is pure." Honesty, sticking to your commitments, keeping promises to yourself and others, doing what you believe is right, and being true to yourself are always the best policies, even if they are not the trend. Trying to be something you are not is guaranteed to make you feel unsure of yourself. Judy Garland put it brilliantly when she said, "Always be a first-rate version of yourself, instead of a second-rate version of someone else."

Be Your Own Best Friend

Hopefully, you are beginning to get the picture by now. Principle #1 is all about discovering your center and being true to yourself. This sounds much easier than it is, so don't panic if you don't always feel good on the inside; just keep working at it. Whenever you start to feel bad about yourself, try this exercise.

Imagine that you have stepped outside yourself and are standing beside yourself. Become your own best friend. What would you say that would be reassuring, supportive, and comforting? How would you encourage yourself to feel good about yourself? Would you give yourself a hug? Would you tell yourself that you are doing okay and you appreciate how tough life can get, but you think you are terrific and coping really well?

This exercise is easy and really helpful. When you feel low, become your own best friend and see how much better this helps you feel.

When you think about yourself, what kind of person do you see? Taking a clear look at yourself is hard to do, especially on those days when you feel low. Many of us are self-critical and find many things wrong with ourselves. Many of these negative beliefs hold no foundation in reality. We are not lazy, stupid, worthless, and so on. We learned these beliefs at an early age when we believed literally everything we were told. Until you can change negative beliefs about yourself, you will always doubt yourself.

So train your mind to believe positive things instead. It really is very simple. Every time you feel or think something negative about yourself, become that best friend again and contradict the negative thought with something positive or reassuring. For example, whenever you tell yourself you are stupid, stop and tell yourself instead that you are intelligent. Keep doing this until it becomes a habit. This technique takes time and practice, but it really does work.

So from now on don't believe everything you think about yourself; challenge it. What have you got to lose? Just a lifetime of self-doubt.

How Do You Like Your Chocolate?

Watch people when they choose a chocolate from a box, or better still, be conscious of how you go about it.

Do you take forever to choose, or do you just grab one without looking? Do you read the selection card first? Noticing these things can give you clues about the way you approach life. Do you eat chocolate quickly or slowly, savoring every moment? What do you think this says about you? What does it mean when you choose the same chocolate over and over again? Are you stuck in a rut, not willing to try something new, or do you simply know what works best for you? Do you take chocolates from the lower tray before the top one is finished? This could indicate that you aren't happy with what life has placed in front of you, or you could be looking for that hidden meaning to life. The principles of chocolate wisdom show you that if you don't find it within you'll never find it, so take your time with chocolate to discover your inner truth.

Remember, You Are Unique

Never forget that you are a unique and special human being—and there is no one quite like you. Think about it. With the possible exception of identical twins, your fingerprints and your DNA are completely different from everyone else's. This means that out of the billions of men and women in the world, you are one of a kind.

Mother Nature has taken the trouble to make you completely unique. So isn't it time that you realized that you have something special to offer—and that you have a right to be here? Isn't it time that you stopped thinking your opinions didn't matter? Start thinking of yourself, with your unique fingerprints and DNA, as someone who matters and who is special.

You are unique. There never has been and never will be another person on this planet who is just like you. This makes you original and special. Now here's a belief that can be comforting when life gets difficult.

Why not enhance your originality? Whenever you feel the urge to fit in, look carefully at whatever it is that makes you different, and celebrate your unique qualities. They are what make you an original person with your own special place in the world.

All too often we go through life comparing ourselves with others, thinking that others are better or thinner or happier or richer or more successful or intelligent or perfect than we are. However, the truth is that nobody is perfect—not you, not me, not anybody. So you are on a par with everyone else. You are not perfect, but you are uniquely special. Your life matters.

All human beings struggle with self-esteem—yes, even those supremely confident folks. It seems as if our self-esteem is always on the line, and our confidence may go up and down with alarming speed. Try not to let the ups and downs get to you. Our self-esteem is rather like a beautiful but delicate flower, and it needs constant nourishment and care in order to grow strong and radiant.

Principle #1 is discovering your self-worth. Use some of the tips here to increase your good feelings about yourself, but as you do, remember that working on your personal development is a lifetime's job. As you cultivate ways to feel better about yourself, your self-esteem will become more constant. Next time you feel disheartened, you will be able to pick yourself up quickly, dust yourself off, and start over again.

Keep working on your self-esteem, and one day something amazing will happen. You'll be able to look deep within yourself, your center, and start liking what you see. You'll feel powerful and alive, and life will feel creative and rewarding. And, rather like that wonderful union between your favorite center and favorite chocolate, nothing feels or tastes as good.

Let It Melt in Your Mouth

ABOUT CHOCOLATE: The next time you eat your favorite chocolate really take your time with it. Let it sit in your mouth for a few seconds before you chew, to release its primary aromas. Then, chew it a few times to release its secondary aromas. Next let it rest lightly against the roof of your mouth so that you experience the full range of flavors and textures. Now, close your eyes, if they aren't shut already, and let the chocolate work its magic.

ABOUT LIFE: Choose the kind of life you want, and live it with courage and passion. Make your life extraordinary.

hocolate is a consuming passion the world over. What if we could devour life with the same kind of commitment and passion?

You Are the Power and the Passion

Principle #1 was all about discovering your self-worth and finding ways, apart from chocolate, to boost good feelings about yourself. Now it's time to take things one stage farther. Principle #2 urges you to become the power, the passion, and the force in your own life—to be as passionate about life as you are about chocolate.

There are two types of people in the world—those who take responsibility and those who blame. Those who make it happen and those who get happened to. Those who are passionate and those who are lackluster. Those who are proactive and those who are reactive.

Happy people are proactive people. They are the captains of their own lives. They choose their attitudes and are passionate about what they believe in. They recognize that they are responsible for their own happiness or unhappiness. Unfulfilled people are reactive people. They allow their happiness or unhappiness to be determined by other people, things, or events. They feel that they don't have any control over their lives.

Want to know more? Compare the following responses to this scenario. You have bought an expensive box of your favorite chocolates, but when you open it at home the quality isn't good.

Reactive choices:

❋ Lose your temper, call the shop, and tell the salesperson the shop sucks.

❋ Blame it on your bad luck. After all, this kind of thing always happens to you.

❋ Comfort yourself with ten bars of cheaper chocolate.

Proactive choices:

❋ Return to the shop and ask for a refund.

❋ Decide not to buy chocolates from that shop again.

❋ Remind yourself to always check the quality the next time you buy expensive chocolates.

You can usually hear the difference between proactive and reactive people by the types of language they use. Reactive people say things like, "That's just me," or "That's the way I am," or "If only this or that had or had not happened." What they are really saying is, "I can't change. I'm not responsible; other people are. I'm not in control; other things are." Notice how reactive language takes power away from you and gives it to someone or something else.

Proactive language, by contrast, puts control back in your hands. Instead of "I can't do it," they say "I'll try." Instead of "That's the way I am," they say "I'm open to trying something new." Instead of "There's nothing I can do," they say "Let's explore all the options." Instead of "I have to," they say "I choose to."

Being proactive means taking responsibility for your life and having a can-do attitude. It means making things happen rather than having them happen to you. It means thinking about solutions and options rather than barriers and problems. It means looking for challenges and opportunities not problems. It means being passionate about your life and seizing the initiative. If you are feeling bad because you feel lonely, don't just wait for the doorbell to ring. Find ways to meet people. Be friendly. Smile more. Ask someone out. People may not know what a great person you are. Don't wait for the perfect job to come to you, go after it. Send out your resume, network, volunteer to gain experience, and so on. This isn't being pushy or aggressive; it's being courageous, persistent, and enterprising.

Turn Rejection into Resolve and Setbacks into Opportunities

So far we've seen that being proactive involves responding to situations in a productive way and taking responsibility for the choices you make. Basically, it means doing all that you can to create the kind of life you want and keeping your cool when the going gets tough. This isn't always easy, but remember, nobody is perfect. Just get into the habit of being proactive. If you are already doing it three times out of ten, try doing it five times out of ten. Never underestimate the big difference that small changes can make.

But what if life deals you a really bad hand? Things don't work out as planned, you are rejected, you make a mistake, you fail, or someone says no. Once again, it is up to you to control how you respond. Be proactive. Setbacks are going to happen in life. It's up to you to turn rejection into resolve.

The first thing to do is to stop blaming yourself. Blame and guilt leave you trapped in the past and won't change anything for the better. Although it's important to accept the part you played in the setback, don't get things out of proportion.

People who are happy with themselves take defeat and view it as an isolated incident that indicates nothing about their ability. People who are unhappy take defeat and enlarge it. They're sure it stands for who they are, and they use it to predict everything about their future. So accept yourself as you are. This doesn't mean ignoring your faults or not taking responsibility; it means believing in your own value even when you make mistakes.

If you can see clearly where you went wrong, use that information and move on, but if you don't know what went wrong or why something happened, stop thinking it's your fault.

Sometimes things just happen in life. Don't take it personally. Perhaps someone is ignoring you not because they dislike you but because they can't focus on anything else but their financial worries. Sometimes relationships don't work out because you have grown apart, and it isn't anybody's fault.

The next time you face disappointment, resist the temptation to blame yourself. Try instead to find out what went wrong. Then, you can try again using what you have found out.

Sometimes, even though we're being proactive, there are things over which we have no control—the weather, the stock market, our age, for example. When that's the case, learn to let go. It makes no sense trying to change things that you have no control over. What matters is how you respond. You can worry and fret (which will achieve nothing), or you can learn to live with it and focus your energy on things that you can do something about.

Every time you experience a setback, it's an opportunity to learn and grow. You have the power within you to rise above whatever happens. Happy people worry less about failing and think more about the chances they will miss if they don't even try.

Every lasting success involves setbacks and disappointment. When you understand this, rejection isn't so frightening anymore—it's an opportunity to be proactive and take a step on the road to success. Be passionate and persistent in a creative way. If you truly want something, you will find ways to get it. Don't give up. Believe in yourself. Anyone who is anyone has had to look rejection in the face. You can too.

When life says no, think of it as, "Not this way, let's look for another." If a diet isn't working, try a nutritionist. If you didn't get a promotion, consider other work opportunities. Don't limit yourself to one way of getting what you want. Be ingenious. Try other approaches—even bold ones, not the way things are usually done. Nothing eases disappointment faster than new challenges.

There will be times, of course, when, despite all your efforts, you can't get what you want. The man or woman of your dreams turns out to be a nightmare, the promotion you are after isn't going to happen, you aren't ever going to squeeze into a size ten, and so on. When you feel you are at the end of the road and you have exhausted all possibilities, push the pause button for a while, treat yourself to a chocolate or two, and take time to reflect. Life isn't going according to your plans, but maybe— just maybe—there is a better plan. It is still possible to look ahead with optimism. Who knows what the future holds?

When you hit an obstacle and can't get past it, get curious about what lies ahead for you. You never know what could be waiting around the corner! Something even better could be just out of sight. That's the way the world works—if you believe it does.

Emotional Confidence

It's hard to be proactive if your emotions are getting in the way of making sound decisions. Perhaps you wake up in the morning feeling sad and that stops you making the most of and enjoying your day. Perhaps someone cuts in front of you in traffic, and you lose your temper and take that irritable attitude with you to work. Perhaps you feel guilty because you haven't stuck to your healthy eating plan, so you throw caution to the winds and eat a whole box of chocolates in one sitting.

If your feelings are making you act in ways that run counter to your values, this can mess up your life. But if you can manage your feelings, you will be more consistent in the way you react and behave. Because you are aware of the influence your feelings have on your ability to think clearly, you will find it easier to be proactive and seek positive rather than negative solutions to setbacks.

It may seem hard to believe, but when you feel at the end of your tether, your feelings cannot make you act in a certain way. They can influence you, yes, but they can't control how you respond. This is important, so I'll repeat it. Your feelings cannot make you act in a certain way unless you allow them to. You are in charge of your feelings; your feelings are not in charge of you.

Reconnecting with and managing your emotions won't be

easy if you have been used to denying them or suppressing them, or giving in to them, so it is important that you start to become more aware of what you are feeling. Your emotions are messages that come from your inner wisdom, and it is important to acknowledge them and feel them. If you suppress them, the biochemical effect is to raise your stress levels. So-called negative emotions, such as fear, anger, or sadness, are not bad emotions; they are necessary for us to grow and develop. Emotions are the only real way we have to show what matters to us and what doesn't. Difficult emotions signal the need for some kind of change in our lives. They require us to act, to change the situation or mind-set that is causing distress, to move on with our lives.

Accept, Choose, and Manage

Once you become more aware of your feelings and have allowed yourself to feel them, it's time to deal with them. Understanding why you are feeling a certain way may help, but remember that sometimes you won't know why. At times you may feel confused, not sure of what you're feeling, and it's then that you are most likely to find yourself reacting inappropriately in certain situations. For example, a delayed train may make you feel wild with anger, or a sad film or song may plunge you into the depths of sadness. Here are a few suggestions to help you cope.

When you begin to notice that your emotions are hurting you or someone else or that you are eating way too much chocolate because you feel low or out of control, remind yourself that you are in charge of your feelings, your feelings are not in control of you. Nothing can make you feel angry, sad, guilty, or frightened unless you allow it to.

Think about what your feelings are trying to tell you. Try to understand the feeling and take responsibility for it, even if that feeling is troublesome or embarrassing. For instance, if you feel sad, don't deny that you're feeling sad or blame other people for making you feel that way. Just notice that you are feeling sad and accept it. Perhaps there is a reason for your sadness, perhaps there isn't. Whatever the case, accept your feelings. Own them.

Recognize too that emotional confusion can be caused by feelings from the past leaking into your present situation. For instance, if your first partner was unfaithful, you may become extremely jealous of your current partner even if he or she is giving you no cause.

Once you have acknowledged your feeling, the next step is to choose how you respond to that emotion. You may wish to try inducing a state of calm within yourself. That way, when you act, you are acting out of your whole self rather than just out of the emotion. For instance, when you feel sad, it can help to have a good cry or talk to a friend or just spend time alone.

Finally, you need to manage the destructive habit that encourages your feelings to overwhelm and confuse you. Throughout the process, remind yourself that managing your feelings can only enrich your experience of life. Feeling something is far, far preferable to feeling nothing at all.

Sadness, Disappointment, and Generally Feeling Low

When you feel emotional, all you may want to do is reach for a chocolate bar, but this isn't being proactive—it's being reactive. Sometimes a little bit of comfort and indulgence is all we need, but when your emotions speak to you, the response they need isn't chocolate. Instead of feeling bad about yourself when you feel sad, angry, scared, jealous, guilty, or low, try these suggestions for taking positive action.

❊ Determine the cause if you can.

❊ Release some of the feelings. Have a good cry!

❊ Comfort yourself, and accept the support and comfort of others.

❊ Get a sense of perspective, and try to salvage a positive aspect from the experience.

❊ If you can, find a constructive way to use the experience of your hurt to benefit yourself or others.

❊ If you can, forgive who or what was responsible for

the hurt, even if it was you, and put the hurt firmly behind you.

❄ If the feelings of sadness become too overwhelming, seek medical advice.

Guilt

When guilt rules, life isn't about being who you are and doing what you want to do, it is about *shoulds* and *oughts*. We'll explore the powerful role that guilt plays in our life in Principle #3, but for now ponder the following:

❄ Think about what your own values are, not those of others.

❄ Let go of the past.

❄ Keep a sense of perspective.

❄ Remind yourself that guilt and worry won't change anything.

❄ Learn from your mistakes; don't repeat them.

❄ If you hurt someone, make amends if you can.

Shame

When you feel ashamed, it's virtually impossible to feel good about yourself and your life. Here are a few suggestions for dealing with shame:

❄ Acknowledge emotional wounds from the past.

❄ Stop putting yourself down.

- ❖ Focus on your strengths, not on your weaknesses.
- ❖ Be good to yourself.
- ❖ Accept support from others who respect and value you and accept you the way you are.
- ❖ Be yourself, and stop playing a role to be what others expect you to be.
- ❖ Think about what you really want.

Anger

Sometimes it is important to feel anger, but when anger gets out of hand, it can be damaging. Here are a few tips for dealing with anger:

- ❖ Deal promptly with minor threats so that tension doesn't build up.
- ❖ Think about what is worth getting angry about and what isn't.
- ❖ Understand what triggers episodes of anger, and make a plan to counteract that.
- ❖ Boost your self-esteem so that you aren't vulnerable to attack.
- ❖ Practice stress management techniques. (We'll talk more about this later.)
- ❖ Find a way to channel your anger, such as playing sports or starting a new hobby.
- ❖ Pay attention to your social support network.

- ❋ If you did lose your cool, reflect on what went wrong and how you could behave differently next time.

Fear

Fear is one of the most limiting emotions. It stops you doing what you want with your life. When fear threatens to become overwhelming:

- ❋ Practice breathing deeply and slowly.
- ❋ Talk to yourself in a constructive, positive way.
- ❋ Work through fear in small, manageable steps.
- ❋ Rehearse before going into stressful situations so that you are mentally prepared.
- ❋ Imagine yourself being calm, and bring that image to your mind.

Jealousy

Wanting other people to behave in a certain way can poison relationships. If you catch yourself feeling jealous, the following might help:

- ❋ Try to enjoy your relationships instead of constantly analyzing them.
- ❋ If you are rejected, take time to heal and don't blame yourself.
- ❋ Keep your life outside your relationships full and satisfying to promote your self-esteem.

❊ Keep making new friends.
❊ Learn to value the importance of personal space and solitude.

Envy

Wanting things you cannot have can injure self-esteem. The next time you feel envious:

❊ Think about the times you have been lucky and the times life has given you a break.
❊ Think of envy as a piece of information telling you what you really want for yourself. Add this to your personal goals.
❊ If your goals are achievable, see if they merit the attention you are giving them. Do you really want them so badly? If you do, replace envy with realistic, achievable goals for yourself.
❊ If your goals are unachievable, replace them with realistic ones.
❊ Always keep a sense of what you value and what your goals are.

Apathy

If you don't want to make any effort anymore, you can do some things to get back on track:

❊ Keep mentally and physically active.

* Visit new places, meet new people, and do new things.
* Don't accept everything you are told at face value.
* Try to eat healthily, and get enough sleep.
* Sign up for some volunteer work.
* Take a class in something you haven't tried before.
* If you have reached a point where you don't feel anything anymore, you could be suffering from depression. Depression is a medical condition that improves with treatment. Seek medical advice immediately.

Loving Too Much

Try not to confuse love with need. To avoid becoming too dependent on another person or group of people:

* Value the importance of personal space and solitude.
* Nurture yourself.
* Have more than one key relationship.
* Don't neglect everything else when you start a special relationship.
* Be on your guard if a person wants to change you or you want to change someone else.
* Be assertive in your relationships.
* Always remember what you want in a relationship.
* Don't put anyone on a pedestal.
* Respond, don't react.

The next time you find yourself reacting with your emotions instead of taking proactive steps, spend a moment standing back and observing yourself. Remember the stepping-outside-yourself technique in Principle #1?

Now consider your options and remind yourself that you have the power to choose. Say that someone cuts in front of you in traffic. You can react by getting angry and stressed, speeding up or trying to cut that driver off, or you can take a moment to calmly observe the situation and consider the safety of yourself and other drivers, refusing to be intimidated. If someone turns you down for a dinner invitation, you can eat a whole box of chocolates and feel unwell, or you can calmly accept that this time it wasn't right, but next time when you ask someone out, the chemistry might click.

Every day of our lives we are given chances to react or to respond. The more we learn to take a step back before we respond, the calmer and stronger we become. However, the more we continue to react and let ourselves be controlled by our feelings, the weaker and more stressed we will get.

Never underestimate the power of individual choice. The choices you make hold the keys to your happiness and success. Are you someone who reacts, or are you someone who responds? Are you in the driver's seat of your life, or are you just a passenger? Are you eating chocolate because you feel you deserve a treat, or are you eating it because you feel upset or anxious? The choice is always yours.

What Do You Want?

Principle #2 urges you to take charge or your life—to be passionate and proactive about the choices you make. But how can you make the right choices if you don't know what you want or where you are heading? To live your life with passion and commitment, you have to know what you want.

Can you close your eyes and visualize where you want to be in ten or fifteen years' time? If all you are getting is a hazy blur, it's time to start thinking about where you are heading.

Perhaps you don't want to think about the future. Do you like living in the present and going with the flow? Living in the present is great; we need to enjoy the now because it's all we've got. But just going with the flow can present a problem. You can end up going where the flow goes—which usually is downhill. You may find yourself doing what other people want you to do or what everybody else is doing, which may not be good for you at all. Never assume that the herd knows where it is going; it usually doesn't.

Basically, most of us just want to be happy, but do we know what that means? If you were granted one wish, do you know what your wish would be? Happy people generally know what they want and feel they are moving in the direction of getting it. That's what makes them happy. They feel they are headed toward something they are passionate about. If you don't know what you want—if you don't know what you are working toward or where you are going—how on earth are you supposed to get there? How will you know what choices to make and what actions to take?

If I asked you to name your favorite chocolate, I bet you wouldn't hesitate. You'd know. When you went shopping, you'd look for it to make sure that you got what you wanted, wouldn't you? So why not be as sure about what you want in your life? It will help you avoid a lot of disappointment.

What's Your Chocolate?

Can the kind of chocolate you like tell you something about yourself and what you want in life? Maybe.

Are you a white chocolate lover, or do you prefer the rich, deep taste of dark chocolate or the silky texture of the smoothest milk chocolate?

White chocolate: White chocolate may contain a good percentage of cocoa butter, but it's not a real chocolate. It is sold for its sweetness and has around 50 percent sugar.

Although many chocolate lovers enjoy it, chocoholic purists would probably avoid it.

Knowing what you want out of life can be a problem for white chocolate lovers. You are capable of many things, but which one will you choose? Forever weighing the pros and cons, you can see all sides of an argument, but when you finally decide what you do want, nothing can stop you.

Milk chocolate: Milk chocolate, like white chocolate, may be avoided by chocoholic purists, because it contains only about 20 percent cocoa butter in cheap brands and around 40 percent in more expensive brands. (Real chocolate should have at least 60 percent.) Nonetheless, it is the chocolate of choice for millions of chocolate lovers around the world.

If milk chocolate is your favorite, there is a part of you that, like Peter Pan, never wants to grow up and leave childhood behind. You love things to be simple, sweet, happy, and straightforward. Your truly young-at-heart approach to life suggests the possibility of greatness. The only danger is an unwillingness to take responsibility for your actions.

Dark chocolate: Also known as plain or bittersweet, dark chocolate has a high cocoa butter content—around 70 percent—and a low sugar content. It may also contain extract of real vanilla and no artificial flavoring. Yes, you guessed it—it's the chocolate of choice for chocoholic purists.

If dark chocolate is your favorite, you are forward thinking and optimistic and have a fertile and active mind that is forever searching for answers. Just try to make sure that your excitement about what the future holds doesn't mean that you neglect the wonder of the present. You are often an expert in your chosen field and have a clear idea about what you want out of life. Although your focus is commendable, it can mean that you have a tendency to be inflexible in your dealings with others.

Every kind of chocolate: You are a flexible person who prides yourself on the ability to fit in anywhere, anytime. Not one to get stuck in a rut, you move with the times and never get left behind. If you can keep a sense of your own identity amid this constant change, you will make your mark on the world.

You probably have a good idea of what you don't want, but can you say what you do want? To be happy, you need to have a good idea of what your ideal life is. You are the driver of your life, and so it is important that you decide where you want to go and how you are going to get there. This doesn't mean deciding every detail of your life, such as where you are going to live or whom you are going to work for; it means deciding in which direction you want your life to go so that each step you take from now on helps you achieve your destiny.

Think about what makes you happy. Think money is the answer? Prosperity is related not to how much money you have in the bank, but to how rich you feel your life is. Research has shown that what people like most about their work or chosen role in life isn't money or status but self-respect. Money can make life easier, but it isn't the determining factor in happiness. Ask any young lover, first-time mother, or Olympic athlete.

Still aren't sure? Here are some questions that you might like to ask yourself. They won't give you an answer overnight, but they might help you think about what inspires you.

* Imagine that you have passed away and a reporter has been asked to write your life history. What would it say?
* If you could spend an hour with anyone—alive, dead, famous, not famous—who would that be and why? What is it about that person that is so exciting?

❀ If you won the lottery and could spend the next year doing anything you wanted, what would it be?

❀ Imagine that you have gone missing and a television crew wants to interview your friends and family about you. What would they say?

❀ Is there something that represents you or something that you have a particular affinity with—an animal, a precious stone, a painting? Why does it represent you?

❀ If a song was written about you, what would it be called?

❀ If a book was written about your life, what would be the title?

❀ List five talents you have. Are you a good listener? Are you good with numbers? Good at observing? Good with your hands? Good at sports? Good at sharing? Good at organizing? Do you have a good memory?

❀ Which of your friends do you admire most and why?

❀ Who do you envy most and why?

❀ Go back to the first ten years of your life. What were you really passionate about then?

❀ Say you had to take up two evening classes a week in subjects you knew very little about, what would they be?

❀ If you could go back in time and talk to your fifteen-year-old self, what would you say?

By reflecting on questions like these, you can step back from your life and see if there are any connections among the things that you enjoy or are intrigued by. What makes you feel really passionate? What makes your heart sing? You'll know when you are onto something because you won't be able to stop thinking about it.

When you do finally settle on something you want, it is easier to make sure that each step takes you in the right direction. Try not to make the mistake of getting fixated on some event, person, or activity you want when what you're really after is the feeling that object, event, person, or activity will give you. For example, say that you want to travel the world. The truth of the matter is that you probably want to have the feelings that come from traveling the world—the freedom and sense of adventure and the excitement of travel. If you are wise enough to realize that what you want are the feelings associated with travel, then you have a number of ways to get that feeling. You can organize regular trips abroad, but you can also get feelings of excitement and freedom from other things, like working freelance, learning a new skill, or learning to hang glide.

If one goal falls by the wayside or just isn't possible, there is no need to feel that you are a loser. Okay, maybe you won't become a brain surgeon, but why not train as a paramedic or even a first-aider? You'll get the same sense of satisfaction and making a real difference in the lives of others. If it doesn't work out one way, don't stop trying to find other ways to make it work. You create your own experience, remember?

Seize the Day

Be passionate about life, and discover a sense of direction and purpose. There is nothing wrong with wanting your life to be special, with working toward your dreams, asking for help with them, and doing all you can to make them happen. And when you do get what you want, for goodness' sake, have the courage to accept it! Principle #1 gave you the strength and resolve to believe that you deserve to be happy. Now it's time for you to be proactive—to step in and say, "Yes, happiness is mine, I want it, I've worked for it, and I deserve it." Be as greedy for and passionate in the pursuit of happiness as you are for chocolate.

Life is short, so why not make yours extraordinary? You don't have to change the world to lead an extraordinary life. What distinguishes an extraordinary person from an ordinary person is passion. Extraordinary people make the most of each day, and however mundane their tasks, they do them to the best of their ability and with a sense of purpose. Most of us won't do great things, such as ensuring civil rights for all or ending world hunger, but we can do small things with passion and by so doing make our valuable contribution to the rich tapestry of life.

Principle 3

Chocolate Makes You Feel Good

~

ABOUT CHOCOLATE: Guilt often goes hand in hand with enjoying this delicious treat. However, recent studies suggest that far from being bad for you, chocolate in moderation can protect your heart, boost your mood, and even help you live longer.

ABOUT LIFE: Stop feeling guilty. Replace *should* with *could*.

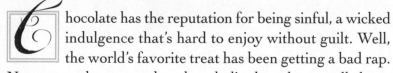 hocolate has the reputation for being sinful, a wicked indulgence that's hard to enjoy without guilt. Well, the world's favorite treat has been getting a bad rap. New research proves what chocoholics have known all along. Chocolate doesn't cause all the problems it's accused of, such as acne, obesity, and even addiction. In fact, eaten sensibly, chocolate has health benefits. Yes, you can indulge without feeling guilty. Why not try letting go of the guilt in your daily life too?

Let Go of the Guilt

In Principle #1, you learned about the importance of building your self-esteem. Guilt can destroy your sense of self-worth. In Principle #2, you learned about the importance of living your life with passion. Guilt can take the passion and the momentum out of your life. And aren't guilt and chocolate closely associated?

There are many negative misconceptions about chocolate, and these misconceptions translate into guilt. Most of the chocolate beliefs that we have today are based on popular myth, not fact. We have to stop living under this persecution. Chocolate is a fundamental part of our lives, so why not have fun with it? That's why Principle #3 urges you to let go of the guilt—and not just when it comes to chocolate, but in every aspect of your life. Guilt disempowers you. It stops you from moving forward, taking risks, having fun, and becoming the kind of passionate and exciting person you want to be.

Do you feel guilty when you say no?
Do you think you aren't good enough?
Do you do things because you feel you ought to, not
   because you want to?
Is it hard for you to let go and have fun?

If you answered yes to any of the above questions, guilty feelings are stopping you from enjoying your life to the fullest. Guilt burns away your self-respect. Many of us are so wracked with guilt that we rush around trying to be all things to everybody, and all the while our self-esteem sinks lower and lower.

People are quick to pick up on guilt; they'll move in to make extra demands on you when they sense any hint of it. If this sounds familiar, it's vital that you stop and take a good long look at the way you are leading your life. Guilt will destroy your chances of happiness unless you decide to do something about it. There are no half measures here. If you want to lead a happy, fulfilling life, there can't be any room for guilt. That's why Principle #3 is all about getting rid of it.

Visualize Your Guilt as a Balloon

It might help to visualize guilty feelings blowing away like a balloon that has been released, never to be seen again. Let go of your balloon, and don't think about it again. Tell yourself that you are doing the best you can, and remind yourself that every time you allow yourself to feel guilty, your chances of happiness grow smaller. Keep practicing letting go of guilt, and the more you do it, the happier your life will become.

A Little of What You Love

Many nutritionists think the effects of the mood-boosting chemicals in chocolate are relatively small and it's more the associations we make with chocolate—warmth, comfort, and indulgence—that make it enjoyable. But although eating chocolate makes us feel good initially, as a recent survey by mental-health charity MIND highlighted, for many of us guilt quickly follows. This is because we see chocolate as bad food and so believe we should restrict our intake or, worse still, avoid it completely. Yet this only makes us crave it more, and we end up declaring ourselves chocoholics.

Why not avoid the guilt, remind yourself that chocolate has got a lot of good things going for it, and enjoy small amounts as part of a balanced diet?

Replace *Should* with *Could*

Have a good long think about all the things you feel you should do. For example, do housework each day, lose weight, be nicer to people, read more, do more, and so on. Now think about these things again, and ask yourself why you should do these things. You may be surprised with the answers. For example, you think you should do housework every day because that's what your mother did, or you think you should be nicer because if you don't people won't like you anymore. But you aren't your mother, and if you are interacting with people because you want them to like you, that's a shaky foundation to base your social life on. Your answers to the "Why should I?" questions show you how you can limit yourself by holding certain beliefs. Question those beliefs.

The word *should* implies guilt and reluctance. Do you really need to burden yourself in this way? From now on, whenever you think that you should or ought to do something, understand that you are putting yourself in the wrong for no reason. Replace *should* with *could*, and start each statement with "If I really wanted to . . ." When you do this, you might find some things you want to do differently. For example, if you really wanted to, you could clean the house every day, but is this how you want to spend your time? Don't be a "should" victim trapped by guilt. Allow yourself the possibility of "could," and let positive change into your life.

Stop Trying to Be Perfect

The notion of perfection often gets in the way of happiness. When something is perfect, it is faultless. We talk of a perfect square or a perfect right angle. But trouble arises when we imagine that we can transfer this exactness to our lives, other people, and human nature. This can't be done. In life there is no exact measurement for what is right. We are not science or statistics.

In human terms, perfection is about being imperfect. It's about being the best we can be, not the best we could be if we were machines without emotions. Stop and ask yourself where your notion of perfection comes from. Real life isn't like the movies or the fairy tales of childhood—and that is what makes it rich and wonderful. If everything were perfect and we never made mistakes, how would we learn and grow? How could we appreciate the good if we didn't experience the bad?

There is nothing wrong with having high standards and ambition, but you do need to be realistic. You are human, after all, and as such are imperfectly perfect. Anyone who is anyone has messed up. We take on a useless burden if we think we are bad just because we make mistakes now and again, just as we rob ourselves of a lot of enjoyment if we think of chocolate as totally bad; see "The Truth about Chocolate" box, which explodes all those chocolate myths. It's okay to make mistakes, have weaknesses, be unpredictable, misunderstand others, and do all the other things that make us human. The issue is keeping a balance so that neither these things nor the search for perfection make us unhappy.

The Truth about Chocolate

Today, we are conditioned to think that chocolate can cause problems such as acne, make you fat, and be bad for your heart, but five hundred years ago it was believed that chocolate had medicinal properties. It was used to rebuild strength, boost mood, stimulate the nervous system, and improve digestion. Nowadays, it is considered more of a comfort food than a health enhancer. However, recent research at the University of California at Davis seems to indicate that eaten in moderation, chocolate can be good for us. Here we explore the myths and truths about chocolate.

Myth: Chocolate raises cholesterol levels.
Fact: Saturated fat in food is one of the main causes of high

cholesterol. According to the British Heart Foundation, chocolate contains about 500 calories per 100 grams and contains 30 percent fat—18 percent of it saturated. The primary saturated fat found in chocolate is stearic acid, which doesn't cause blood cholesterol to rise.

Myth: Chocolate doesn't contain vitamins or minerals.
Fact: Chocolate is a good source of magnesium—especially important for women—potassium, manganese, vitamin A, phosphorus, and calcium, plus traces of iron, zinc, and copper.

(Women only) constant cravings: If you've ever had a chocolate craving before your period, you could be hankering after magnesium. During the seven days before a period, the level of magnesium in your blood falls, which causes chemical imbalances and mood swings. Evidence suggests that consuming more magnesium prior to menstruation may help correct imbalances. But choose the best chocolate you can buy, because that has the highest magnesium count.

Myth: Chocolate triggers migraines.
Fact: Cheese can cause a migraine because it contains large

quantities of tyramine. Chocolate, however, contains only small quantities of tyramine and shouldn't be unfairly blamed.

Myth: Chocolate causes tooth decay.
Fact: Chocolate contains fermentable carbohydrates. These are present in most starches and sugars and have the potential to cause tooth decay. However, milk chocolate has a high content of protein, calcium, phosphate, and other minerals that can protect tooth enamel. Cocoa and chocolate also have the ability to offset the acid-producing potential of the sugar they may contain.

Myth: Chocolate makes children hyperactive.
Fact: Research by the U.S. Food and Drug Administration has found that chocolate eaten in moderation does not cause hyperactivity in children or adults.

Myth: Chocolate is high in caffeine.
Fact: Caffeine is thought to artificially stimulate the system and can temporarily increase your level of adrenaline. People often reach for a cup of coffee or a bar of chocolate, but ounce for ounce chocolate appears far better for

you than a cup of coffee. The amount of caffeine in a piece of chocolate is significantly lower than that in coffee, tea, or cola drinks. For example, an 8-ounce cup of instant coffee has between 10 and 40 milligrams of caffeine, while a 1-ounce chocolate bar contains only 6 milligrams.

Myth: Chocolate causes acne.
Fact: Studies by the Pennsylvania School of Medicine found that acne is not linked to chocolate consumption. Researchers there found that the culprit was hormonal fluctuations.

Myth: Chocolate is addictive.
Fact: Experts say that we crave chocolate not because of its chemical properties but because it's so magnificently sensuous. Studies show that people crave chocolate because of the intense pleasure of eating it, not because it is physiologically addictive.

It's Okay to Say No

How often do you agree to do something that you don't want to do? Do you feel guilty when you say no? If you say yes when you mean no, you are denying your own needs and inviting other people to victimize you. But why is it so hard to say no?

Saying no is a problem for most people because the word is linked with behavior that is described as thoughtless, uncaring, or mean. To say it creates the risk that the other person will feel rejected and won't like you anymore, and if other people don't like you, that makes you feel worthless.

If you find it hard to say no, your major preoccupation is with what people will think of you, and you are likely to do anything to ensure that people like you. Whatever happened to your feeling of self-worth? It's being strangled by limiting beliefs about yourself. It's time to ditch those beliefs and stop acting like a victim.

Think about this: When you say no, it simply means that you don't want to do what you are being asked to do; it doesn't mean that you are rejecting someone as a person. Likewise, if someone says no to you, it does not mean that that person is rejecting you.

Whenever you are afraid to say no, think about the true meaning of your communication. Remember, you are not rejecting the other person. It's okay to say no. *No* is not a dirty word. The wonderful thing about learning to say no is that the more you do it, the easier it gets. Try saying it in a way that is not hurtful. Offer an explanation, express your feelings, and offer an alternative—but if the other person feels rejected, this isn't your fault. Keep your resolve. If you feel sorry or guilty, remember your intention. Don't apologize for your *no* and wait for the other person to accept it. Remember, you are not rejecting the other person. You are only saying no.

Chocolate Can Lift Your Spirits

Chocolate contains a number of chemicals, including tryptophan, tyrosine, and phenylalanine, which are believed to trigger the release of endorphins, the natural feel-good hormones, in the brain. These create feelings of pleasure similar to those experienced when we fall in love. Plus it contains small amounts of caffeine, a stimulant that can reduce feelings of fatigue and increase alertness. Researchers have also found that physical and emotional enjoyment, even in small doses, can boost your immune function for hours afterward. They believe that life's small pleasures have a cumulative effect in boosting the immune system long-term.

It's Okay to Say Yes

It's okay to say yes to things that might appear silly, indulgent, or plain selfish to other people. If your to-do list gets so long that you feel overwhelmed, it's okay to go for a walk, lock your-self in your room for a good cry, take a long soak in a warm bath, indulge in a chocolate milkshake—whatever it takes to clear your head. And if you feel you need a treat, it's okay to say yes to that shopping trip, that weekend away, an afternoon in a bookstore, a chocolate cake for dessert. Life wouldn't be worth living without time for pleasure. Don't let guilt stop your having fun or taking time out now and again. You deserve it.

Regularly having fun is one of the five central factors in lead-ing a satisfied life—the other four being good health, good self-esteem, having a sense of control over your life, and being valued by others. Studies have shown that people who spend time enjoying themselves are more likely to feel happy on a daily basis.

Pleasure plays an important part in daily life, but it is under-valued and underexplored in both science and society, accord-ing to ARISE (Associates for Research into the Science of Enjoyment), an organization that was established in order to create a better understanding of the benefits of pleasure and the important part it plays in a balanced and well-rounded approach to life. Pleasure is important to health in two ways. First, it can act proactively to promote good physical and mental health and protect against illness. Second, it can aid the process of unwinding and reduce the stress of recent unpleasant experi-ences. Research shows that experiencing pleasure leads to a reduction in the stress hormones, such as cortisol, and strengthens the immune response, therefore offering us greater resistance to infections and disease.

Take some time this week to plan ahead for pleasure. Don't limit yourself to just one source, such as chocolate; there are hundreds and thousands of other ways to get pleasure. Perhaps you have a hobby, sport, or leisure pursuit that is a steady source of pleasure. If you don't know what you enjoy, you might have to do a little detective work to find out. You might like to try an evening class, do some volunteer work, ask other people what they enjoy, or plan an afternoon or evening where you try something you have never done before, just because it sounds interesting—such as rock climbing, belly dancing, or having a full-body massage. By doing this you can start to see if there are connections among things you enjoy or feel energized by. Think about those dreams that you have put aside because other things got in the way. Are you ready to revisit them?

Don't worry if you find that your interests change as you get older. Sometimes we just outgrow things and need to find new ones to energize us all over again. The important thing isn't so much what you are doing but the spirit in which you are doing it. Are you having fun on a regular basis?

> Chocolate is a perfect food, as wholesome as it is
> delicious, a beneficent restorer of exhausted power;

but its quality must be good, and it must be carefully prepared. It is highly nourishing and easily digested, and it is fitted to repair wasted strength, preserve health, and prolong life. It agrees with dry temperaments and convalescents, with mothers who nurse their children, with those whose occupations oblige them to undergo severe mental strains, with public speakers, and with all those who give to work a portion of the time needed for sleep. It soothes both stomach and brain, and for this reason, as well as for others, it is the best friend of those engaged in literary pursuits.

— Baron von Liebig, German chemist
and educator (1803–1873)

Sweet News for Moms

Pregnant women can tuck into Easter eggs in the knowledge that it may help their babies. Scientists have discovered that expectant mothers who eat a lot of chocolate have happier and more active babies. Their children will be less stressed than those born to women who abstained. The

University of Helsinki study, reported in *New Scientist* magazine, asked more than 300 pregnant women to rate their stress levels and chocolate consumption. Not only were the babies born to women who ate chocolate daily in pregnancy more active, but they also smiled and laughed more often.

So it's official—pleasure is essential in your life and good for your health and well-being. Chocolate is an enormous source of pleasure, and as long as you remember to eat it in moderation, there is no need to feel guilty. So relax when you indulge, and let the good feelings chocolate promotes work their magic. And if you want an easy way to practice guilt-free indulgence, try the recipes in the appendix at the back of this book.

Forgive Yourself

Forgiveness is a powerful way to feel better. Forgiving others doesn't mean it's okay for them to do nasty things to us. Forgiving, instead, is about letting go of guilty, angry, and resentful thoughts that you may have so they don't drag you down. Forgiveness is not about overlooking, but about moving on.

But who do we find hardest to forgive? Why, ourselves, of course. We are our own harshest critics. Can we ever be good enough, clever enough, slim enough? When we are low in confidence, we become our own worst enemy and end up feeling worse and worse. Self-forgiveness is one of the keys to personal power. When you can stop feeling guilty that you aren't perfect or good enough, and you can love and value yourself despite your shortcomings, you are free to be yourself and reach your highest potential.

So stop feeling guilty. Stop beating yourself up. Break the critical habit, which is such a waste of your precious time. It's okay to say yes. It's okay to say no. It's okay to enjoy chocolate. It's okay to have fun. It's okay to enjoy your life. Let go of guilt. Let go of self-blame. Forgive yourself—and free yourself.

Healthy Heart, Long Life

There is evidence that eating chocolate as part of a balanced diet may help to keep the heart and circulation healthy. In fact, chocolate is being taken so seriously as a potential heart protector that it was discussed at length during the 2001 Congress of the European Society of Cardiology, and studies on the protection chocolate may offer against heart disease have been published in the British medical journal *Lancet*.

It seems chocolate's protective action comes from substances found in cocoa solids which act as antioxidants. Antioxidants can help prevent harmful cholesterol from being deposited in the arteries, thus reducing the risk of heart disease. But that's not all. Eating chocolate regularly may contribute to a lower risk of blood clots, says Carl Keen, professor of nutrition and internal medicine at the University of California. This is so because the compounds found in cocoa appear to have an aspirin-like effect, improving circulation and making blood less likely to clot—all good news for those at risk from heart attack, stroke, or deep vein thrombosis.

Also bear in mind that chocolate might just extend your life. Katharine Hepburn's doctor has suggested that the fact that she ate dark chocolate every day may have contributed or even caused her longevity. The artist Beatrice Wood, who died in 1998, attributed her longevity of 105 years to chocolate and young men. Research by the Harvard School of Public Health found that people who consumed a moderate amount of chocolate survived longer than those who ate a large amount and, more interestingly, longer than those who never touched sweets.

No Need to Eat the Whole Box

ABOUT CHOCOLATE: Chocolate can be good for you, but eat too much of it and it can do more harm than good. As with most things in life, moderation is the key.

ABOUT LIFE: Have the strength to say yes to what is important and no to what isn't.

e're forever being told that chocolate is bad for us, as it's packed with fat and calories, but this is only when you eat too much of it. The secret is knowing when to stop.

Being Strong

> The Spanish ladies of the New World are madly addicted to chocolate to such a point that they are not content to drink it several times a day, they have it served to them in church.
>
> —Anthelme Brillat-Savarin,
> cookbook author (1755–1826)

You're feeling tired. You've had a tough day. You've got to cook supper and sort out the kids' homework. On top of that, you have work to do, the dog needs a walk, and the housework needs to be done. There are several bars of chocolate in the fridge. You could have one to give you a boost, but you want to eat the lot even though you know it isn't good for you. What do you do?

Principle #4—knowing when to stop—can help. It's all about having the willpower and the strength to say yes to things that are good for you and no to things that will set you back.

Reckless Indulgence

Chocolate may have a greater antioxidant capacity than some fruits and vegetables, but it's important to point out that it also contains high levels of saturated fats and sugar, which contribute to high cholesterol, obesity, and coronary heart disease when eaten in excess. We can't just replace our optimum five daily portions of fruits and vegetables with chocolate. So, enjoy a little chocolate in moderation, but ensure that you eat a healthy, balanced diet high in fruits and vegetables to get all the nutrients you need without the added fat.

Stepping out of the Comfort Zone

You've just put a succulent piece of chocolate in your mouth. Mmm. It starts to melt, and the velvety warmth fills you with indescribable pleasure, while the rich familiar aroma holds you in its power. Reluctantly, you swallow. You want another, don't you?

It would be so easy to grab another. You could do it all night. But just think how bad you'd feel after you've had six—or ten.

Knowing when to stop is all about being good to yourself now — and later too.

But sometimes it takes courage to be good to yourself. Doing things that are going to help you in the long run — like stopping when you've had enough to eat or drink, sticking to an exercise routine, applying for a new job, or making new friends — isn't easy. In fact, all of these things can make you feel downright uncomfortable. Crawling out of your comfort zone is full of pressure and uncertainty, so why on earth would anyone want to do it? Because it's the place to go for opportunity — and the only place to find happiness.

Ways to Get Your Chocolate Fix without Piling on the Pounds and the Guilt

1. Try a reduced-fat chocolate dessert.
2. Choose low-fat chocolate bars.
3. Try a low-calorie chocolate drink.
4. Use cocoa powder instead of solid chocolate whenever possible in recipes, so you can get all the taste without the fat.

5. Try chocolate-flavored cereal.
6. Go for chocolate spread; a thin layer on whole-grain toast tastes delicious.
7. Buy fun-size bars — so you won't have to stop after just a bit of a grown-up-size chocolate bar.

You may wonder what is so wrong with staying in your comfort zone. Nothing. Many of us spend a lot of time there. But real exhilaration is found when we stretch ourselves, meet a challenge, do something we didn't think we could do. And to accomplish such things, we need self-discipline.

The Nature of Overindulgence

Chocolate has to be the ultimate comfort food. Many of us turn to it as a way of coping with stress. Rather than dealing with difficult emotions and moving forward with our lives, we reach for a chocolate bar — or two or five or ten. We feel better in the short term, but in the long term we feel worse. Plus, now we've turned chocolate into an enemy — the culprit, we think, of our poor health and weight gain.

Do yourself a big favor. Keep chocolate as a friend — the aphrodisiac of choice, the most sumptuous treat in the world —

by refusing to overindulge. Enjoy a delicious nibble as a pick-me-up. Taste the mouth-watering sensuousness when you are in the right mood with the right person. Enjoy it often in small quantities. That way you'll never consume more of it than is good for you, and you'll never need to use it as a substitute for love.

An Ounce a Day

"My research shows that a diet containing about an ounce of chocolate a day increases good cholesterol and prevents bad cholesterol from oxidizing, a process that may lead to heart disease," says Penny Kris-Etherton, professor of nutrition at Penn State University who recently led a study that found that people who ate a diet rich in cocoa powder and dark chocolate had lower cholesterol levels than those who didn't.

This doesn't mean you should run to the supermarket and fill your cart with chocolate bars for medicinal purposes. You know better than that. It's okay to eat chocolate in small amounts, as long as you eat an otherwise healthy diet and can afford the calories. Try eating it with nuts or fruit for more good fats and even more antioxidants. But don't think you can use chocolate as a replacement for fat-free fruits and vegetables. It just isn't. An ounce of chocolate can contain a whopping 11 grams of fat so you need to compromise elsewhere to make room for the calories. But if you eat your 1-ounce (28-gram) piece of chocolate slowly and mindfully, it should satisfy the most serious chocolate cravings and help you stick to your healthy eating plan.

So, the message is enjoy a little chocolate but not in excess. One bar of chocolate, not the whole box. A few chocolate chip cookies, not the whole pack. Chocolate dessert one or two times a week, not every day. Two or three chocolates from a selection, not twenty. Know when to stop.

When One Is Never Enough

If you can't restrain yourself as far as chocolate is concerned or if eating makes you feel guilty, you could be developing an unhealthy relationship with food, and it's important to get back on track. You may find the steps below helpful. You'll see that the focus here is on understanding your relationship with food—chocolate in particular—so that you can move forward in life. But the advice here could apply equally well to any area in life in which you feel you don't have control—fast food, drink, cigarettes, sex, or shopping—because it's all about building your self-esteem. Part of regaining a healthy attitude toward food is separating food from negative feelings about yourself. Once you can do that, you can feel free to enjoy food and know when to stop without feeling deprived.

STEP ONE: RELAXATION

If you feel anxious and long to eat chocolate, one of the most thoroughly tested antianxiety techniques is relaxation. Relaxation can calm the physical signs of anxiety, such as a rapid heartbeat and sweating, and it can also calm you mentally and emotionally. Anxiety is nature's alarm system to help you cope with stressful situations, but too much of it can affect your long-term health.

There are many ways to relax, and you need to find what works best for you. Sitting down in a quiet place where you won't be disturbed, taking slow deep breaths, and gently clenching and relaxing all your muscles, starting with your toes and moving to your shoulders, face, and jaw, can be an enjoyable and easy way to relax. Or you could try the anytime-anyplace-anywhere technique, mentally scanning your body for tense points, exaggerating their tension, and then letting it all go.

You may prefer to go for a long walk or listen to calming music. Whatever it is, it should relax you, free you from tension, and clear your mind so that you can start to think about what you want to achieve.

Slowing down your breathing when you are craving chocolate can also help. The minute you become anxious, your breathing becomes shallower and more rapid, increasing your anxiety. To interrupt this, give yourself a chance to calm down, take slow deep breaths through your nostrils, and focus on your diaphragm as it moves up and down. As a rough guide, aim for four or five seconds for breathing in and four or five more for breathing out.

Meditation can also ease anxiety and stress, perhaps because it shuts off your mind and allows your body to relax. You don't need to join a class or do any fancy techniques; just sit upright, close your eyes, and focus on your breathing. It might help to say a word such as *calm*, *content*, or *peace* quietly to yourself. If unwanted thoughts about chocolate (or alcohol or cigarettes or money or shopping or anything you feel you haven't got control over) intrude, simply notice them and then let them go, as if your thoughts are a handful of sand that runs through your fingers or a bottle of water you are pouring out. Or you could imagine yourself batting them with a tennis racket. For the best results, aim to meditate for 10 to 20 minutes twice a day.

STEP TWO: AWARENESS

Overeating in response to stress and anxiety can become a habit, but like any habit it can be broken. Becoming aware of when you eat, what you eat, and how you eat can help you replace negative habits with positive ones. Then, if you choose to enjoy the odd chocolate bar or glass of wine, you're making a positive choice rather than being driven by underlying emotional tensions. Remember, eating to make the tensions go away is doomed to fail, but dealing with the tensions will help you eat with joy.

Think about when you eat and why. Keeping a food-and-mood diary might help. Remember, this diary isn't about controlling your diet, it is about finding out more information to help you understand your eating habits.

A diary works best if kept in a clear and methodical manner. Find yourself a conveniently sized notebook that you can carry around with you. It works best to write down what you eat and drink at the time you do it, because at the end of the day it can be hard to remember. One suggestion for the layout is given below.

Day:
Time:
How hungry am I before eating?
How do I feel physically?

How do I feel mentally/emotionally?
What I ate:
What I drank:
How hungry am I after eating?
How do I feel physically?
How do I feel mentally/emotionally?

Examples of physical symptoms you could include are: tiredness, headache, stomachache, backache, or weakness. Examples of emotional or mental symptoms are feeling: anxious, irritable, forgetful, unable to concentrate, restless, angry, sad, bored, tearful, or happy. Rating your symptoms provides you with a way of comparing how you feel from one day to another. You may want to give each symptom a score by rating it on a scale from 1 to 5, with 5 being the worst possible feeling and 1 being very mild.

Discovering what chocolate means to you and uncovering your relationship with it will help you understand yourself better. Becoming more aware of your feelings when you eat will also help you become more attuned to hunger signals.

When you eat, focus just on eating; you'll notice when you are full or have had enough, and then you won't have to deal with feeling bloated and overfull. The next time you want to grab a chocolate goodie, ask yourself if you are really hungry.

Ask yourself if something other than food—like a walk, a chat, a hug—would satisfy you instead. If you are hungry, a useful tip is to smell your food first. Smell is the sense most directly linked to the brain, and it's your sense of smell that will help you get back in touch with what your body really needs. You might also try drinking a glass of water, because thirst sometimes gets confused with hunger.

When you do eat, take your time and really think about what you are eating. You'll notice that you recognize sooner when you are full, and you'll also notice when you are eating foods that you don't really enjoy. You may even find that many of the foods you thought you couldn't live without—such as fast foods and snacks—don't actually taste that good. Then, when it comes to eating chocolate, you'll be ready to rediscover the joy of eating something truly delicious.

STEP THREE: REGAIN YOUR BALANCE

Once you become aware that you may be using chocolate and food for a feeling of comfort, you are better placed to make positive changes. For instance, you could start eating chocolate only when you have time to really savor it, you could stop eating when you have had enough, or you could snack on fruit for a change instead. You could phone a friend instead of eating a carton of chocolate ice cream, go for a walk instead of reaching for a packet of chocolate crackers, or watch a favorite video or give someone a hug instead of stocking up with cookies. Choosing to regain your balance means choosing to enjoy food—including chocolate—in moderation. That way you can keep feeling good about yourself instead of feeling like a failure because you overindulged. The next time you are tempted to eat one more chocolate than makes you feel good, pause, take a deep breath, focus on your feelings, and then have the courage to stop.

Finding Your Courage

Every day we are faced with choices—do we do the right thing, or do we take the easy path? Do we get up when the alarm rings, or do we risk running late the whole day? Do we control our temper or say things we later regret? Do we have a few chocolates or the whole box? If you can recognize these key moments and meet them with courage, you will come out victorious.

So, the next time you want to make new friends, apply for a job, break an old habit, get involved, be yourself, or say no to something that isn't good for you, do it! Be strong and clever when the going gets tough. Don't sacrifice your happiness or health for a few moments of indulgence you know you will later regret. You deserve better than that.

Quality Speaks for Itself

How do you recognize high-quality chocolate? Easy: look for 50 to 70 percent cocoa solids in the contents. It will say so on the wrapper. The more cocoa solids, the better the chocolate. Cheap chocolate has only around 10 percent. Also, be sure to check the sugar content. The higher the sugar content—and some can be around 65 percent—the poorer the quality. Very good quality chocolate should be only around 30 percent sugar. Try also to avoid chocolate with vegetable fat and artificial flavoring.

Carob is used as a healthy alternative to chocolate because it does not contain stimulants. It is lower in fat than chocolate and has a higher calcium content, but cocoa is higher than carob in niacin, iron, zinc, phosphorus, and vitamin E. Carob is essentially a low-fat food, but the fat levels of carob foods are substantially increased in production by the addition of coconut oil and hydrogenated vegetable oils.

Another tip: think real cocoa. Joe Vinson, professor of chemistry at the University of Scranton in Pennsylvania, has found that pure cocoa powder (not the instant hot chocolate type) has the most antioxidants, followed by dark chocolate, then milk chocolate.

When you are tempted to do something that's ultimately bad for you, find the discipline to be strong. A man by the name of Albert Gray spent years studying people who were successful and happy to figure out what made them that way. What do you think he found? It wasn't good genes, pushy parents, money, or good looks. It was the ability to do things from time to time that they didn't like. Why? Because they knew that these things would increase their chances of happiness in the long term.

In other words, sometimes you just have to use your willpower to get what you want, whether you like it or not. It isn't easy, but whoever said life should be easy? The only way to learn and grow is to challenge yourself and find your courage and discipline. You may not be aware of it, but every time you stop eating when you've had enough or take the time to get a job done properly, you are a step further on the path to happiness and fulfillment.

A Little Good Chocolate Goes a Long Way

ABOUT CHOCOLATE: Choose the best chocolate you can buy. The higher the quality, the healthier and more satisfying the chocolate.

ABOUT LIFE: Expect nothing less than the best from yourself and your life.

It really is worth your while treating yourself to higher-quality chocolate because it tastes better and is often healthier and purer. But don't stop there. Expect quality in your life. Be honest with yourself: Is your life working? Is it the best that it can be?

> Monseigneur was in his inner room, his sanctuary of sanctuaries, the holiest of holies to the crowd of worshippers in the suite of rooms without. Monseigneur was about to take his chocolate. Monseigneur could swallow a great many things with ease, and was by some few sullen minds supposed to be rather rapidly swallowing France; but, his morning's chocolate could not so much as get into the throat of Monseigneur without the aid of four strong men besides the Cook.
>
> Yes, it took four men, all ablaze with gorgeous decoration and the Chief of them unable to exist with fewer than two gold watches in his pocket, emulative of the noble and chaste fashion set by Monseigneur's lips. One lackey carried the chocolate-pot into the sacred presence; a second milled and frothed the chocolate with the little instrument he bore for that function; a third presented the favored napkin; the forth (he of the two gold watches) poured the chocolate out.
>
> —Charles Dickens, *A Tale of Two Cities*

Are You Treating Yourself with Dignity and Respect?

Be the one who sets the tone in your life. The most important relationship you will ever have, and the one that sets the tone for every other relationship in your life, is the relationship you have with yourself. Everyone in your life will watch how you treat you, what you require of you, and whether or not you are willing to stand up for you. When you treat yourself with dignity and respect, you send a loud and clear message that you are in a position of strength and power.

Think about the way the people in your life are treating you. Are you putting up with things you don't like? What can you do to change the way they treat you? For example, if someone is rude to you, don't just put up with that behavior; complain about it in a calm way.

There is an exception to all this, of course. If someone is physically, mentally, or emotionally abusing you, that is totally different. You did not teach them to do that. It is not your fault, and you need help to change it or escape from it. Get help. Be there for yourself. You are worth it.

So, with the understanding that we are not talking about dangerous, abusive, and violent behavior, let's continue. Teaching other people how to treat you means that you train other people with your reactions. For example, if you are trying to talk to your boss when she is busy with something, and she half ignores you and you just walk away, then you have rewarded your boss by teaching her that if she just ignores you, you will go away.

Change your key actions and reactions, and people will change the way they treat you. It really is as simple as that. You may find resistance at first—old habits die hard—but if you keep trying, things will improve. You are in a position of influence. And the place to begin, as always, is with yourself. Simply by deciding that you will no longer put up with behavior you do not want, you are making a commitment to positive change.

Expect nothing less than the best for yourself, and watch your life immediately change for the better.

> If you refuse to accept anything but the best, you'll get the best. Begin to live as you wish to live.
>
> —Anonymous

Your Chocolate Personality

The shapes you are attracted to when presented with a choice of chocolates might reveal aspects of your personality and the way you appear to others. When using this fun approach to self-analysis, base your choice on instinct or first impressions—take the shape that you naturally want.

Square: Square people tend to be honest and truthful and logical. You like to do things by the book, and you have a tendency to get bogged down with details. You prefer to have a loyal set of long-term friends. Your approach to relationships can be quite old-fashioned, but magic and romance mean a lot to you.

Rectangle: You are loyal and dependable and calming. A great listener, you offer friendship and will go out of your way to help others. Your concentration is brilliant, and studying comes naturally to you. You don't enjoy conflict. In relationships you are loving, tactile, and thoughtful.

Oval: Oval people often have a huge network of friends, as they always seem to have the right word for the right occasion. You work from the heart and go with what you feel, but this can sometimes lead to rash, impulsive decisions, which can get you into trouble. You are not afraid to express your true feelings and are unlikely to remain single for long.

Spiral: Your love of energy and action can sometimes lead to a chaotic lifestyle. You are full of ideas and an eternal optimist who will never hold back and always have a go at new things. Your love life is chaotic too, but when you are committed, you are an exciting and passionate lover.

Circle: Circle people are warm, friendly, and welcoming. You love the company of others and, given a choice, would prefer to be with people rather than alone. You love to socialize and party. There is a tendency to be a people pleaser, and your need to be everyone's best friend may get you overinvolved with other people's problems. You tend to focus on outward appearance. Your challenge is to understand that what goes on in the inside matters far more than outward show.

Triangle: You like to make things happen. You are a great communicator and can talk your way out of any situation. You like to be a leader and make your own rules. Your only downside is self-absorption.

Diamond: You are a person of integrity. You have no time for the superficial. It is important for you to be doing something that you believe in and that will make the world a better place. You love to be surrounded by beauty and, when in a relationship, are deeply committed.

Of course, take these personality hints with a pinch of salt. Circle lovers aren't all sociable, and not everyone who chooses a square is organized, but perhaps the next time you choose or watch someone else choose from a selection box, it might (like the fun discover-your-center exercise in Principle #1) get you thinking about the way you, or they, behave. It's easy to get stuck in a particular role, and it's even easier for other people to expect us to play that role.

High-Quality Thinking

Once you begin to recognize that you owe it to yourself to expect nothing less than the best in every aspect of your life — from the chocolates that you eat to the friends that you have — you can start to make positive changes. You can replace what is second rate with the high quality. And the most important of these changes needs to be in the way you think.

Tasting Chocolate

Experts advise us to eat chocolate on its own—separate from a meal—and to take time to savor it. Oh, and if it's quality, just a little can sate the deepest longings (for chocolate, that is!). Begin first with the smell. Is it rich and not too sweet? Then, listen for the sound. It should snap well when you break it. It should look smooth and clear with no indication of a bloom—a cloudy white residue left on the chocolate when it has been exposed to too much heat. Good chocolate should melt immediately in the mouth if it has not already done so in your hand. Poor-quality chocolate doesn't melt so easily. But it's the taste that is most important. High-quality chocolate should be rich and creamy with just a hint of sweetness, not too much. It should also be slightly bitter, causing a zing in your mouth when you suck it.

Chocolate contains over five hundred different flavors—far more than any other food we eat—which is why it should be tasted slowly. If you give them time, your taste buds can identify all those five hundred flavors, even though you probably won't be able to consciously distinguish them.

So, don't hurry your chocolate. Let your taste buds have time to sort out the flavors so that you can experience them and feel satisfied on a sensual level.

The way you think affects the way you feel. If you think you aren't worthwhile, then you won't feel worthwhile. Try this simple exercise. Think of something really sad, such as a funeral. Now think of a time when you felt really happy, such as a vacation. You will notice immediately how your thoughts affect your feelings.

If you constantly think of yourself in a negative light, thoughts like "I'm useless" or "I can't cope" start to become ingrained. Think negatively for long enough, and you may not even be aware that you are doing it anymore.

Once you start to recognize how negative thought patterns affect the way you feel about yourself, you can start to replace them with other thoughts. You may argue that sometimes negative thoughts are more realistic because life often hands us disappointments. This may have a grain of truth. It's unrealistic to expect positive outcomes to everything. But psychologists and psychiatrists have shown that unhappy people are often biased toward whatever is negative.

Don't believe everything you think. Question it. You don't believe everything other people tell you or what you read in the papers, so why accept everything your thoughts tell you? It's incredible how many inaccuracies are revealed when you start challenging negative thinking.

You don't have to replace negative thoughts with positive ones, just with more appropriate ones. Positive thinking can be as unhelpful and as unrealistic as negative thinking, but fortunately realistic thoughts are much more optimistic than negative ones. Realistic thoughts take into account the negative, but they also take into account other possibilities. For example, saying to yourself, "I'm no good at anything," can be replaced by, "There are things I'm not good at, but there are also things I'm good at."

Most of the time negative thoughts are inaccurate, misleading, and unrealistic because they present only one side of the picture: the negative side.

Just as it's best to go for quality in your chocolate, go for quality in your thinking. The trick is to recognize when you have a negative thought and to ask yourself, "Am I being realistic?" From now on, every time you have negative thoughts about yourself—typical ones are listed below—start challenging them with reason, realism, and facts.

Preserving the Quality

Humidity and heat are chocolate's greatest enemies. Both cause chocolate to bloom, which means small crystals appear on the surface, giving it a whitish or gray appearance. To prevent this, keep chocolate in a cool (slightly warmer than the fridge—around 66–77°F or 19–25°C), dry place. Don't store it below 55°F either, because this will also cause it to bloom. And because chocolate absorbs surrounding odors, it should be kept in an airtight container.

Exaggerating

Self-doubters often make mountains out of molehills. A small setback becomes a major disaster. "I totally messed that up" may refer to a minor mistake; a minor cold is a near-death experience. Exaggerating only makes you feel even more out of your depth. Try to get into the habit of describing situations as they are and not dramatizing them. This will help you feel more in control. Okay, you made a mistake, but this isn't the end of the world. Learn from the experience, apologize if you need to, and move on.

"I've Failed Again"

Everyone makes mistakes. In fact, the most interesting, exceptional people are the ones who make the most mistakes. The only way to learn about your strengths and your weaknesses is to make mistakes. Of course, failures can be devastating, but they can also help you grow and learn about yourself and what you do and do not want in life. You can gain something from every experience, however disappointing. When you hold this attitude, there is no such thing as a failure.

Remember, it's not what happens to you but how you react to what happens to you that determines your self-worth. If you failed an exam, find out what your weakness was and try again. If you didn't get the job you wanted, find out why and use that knowledge to improve your chances at the next job you apply for. Rather than labeling your mistakes or disappointments as failures, try to view them as setbacks or learning experiences, which will add to your store of knowledge. That way you will feel less inclined to give up and more willing to try again.

All or Nothing: "I'm Never Going to Get This Right, So Why Should I Bother?"

Negative thinkers often see life in black-or-white terms. Something is either totally good or totally bad. If something isn't perfect or done to the highest standards, then it isn't worth doing. This kind of thinking sets you up for disappointment and heartache. It is impossible to do something perfectly, especially if you have made only a few attempts at it. There will always be room for improvement, however brilliant you are.

You may think, "What's the point, if I'm not going to be the best at what I do?" The point is that there are a lot of advantages to learning new skills. There are great rewards in getting better and better. If you aren't perfect at something, you can still do it well and get lots of satisfaction from it.

If you catch yourself thinking in all-or-nothing terms, try to challenge the negative thinking by seeing the advantages in your situation. Don't overlook degree or compromise. Perhaps your novel isn't destined to become a literary classic — but it might give you pleasure. Perhaps your presentation wasn't the best that you can do — but it was still effective. Tell yourself, "I didn't get it quite right, but I am getting better all the time."

"That's It; I Can't Do It"

Negative thinkers often get the idea that if something has gone wrong once, it will always go wrong. You have a bad day at work, and you decide that you aren't good at your job. You have an argument with your partner and decide that the relationship is in crisis.

Everywhere you turn you can find examples of setbacks

leading to success. Walt Disney, Steven Spielberg, and J. K. Rowling are just a few examples of people whose ideas were initially rejected but who eventually achieved spectacular success. Sometimes when you are tuning in to a radio station, you get the wrong wavelength. You keep fiddling with the tuner until you get the quality of reception that you want. Persistent effort pays off. Just because you didn't get the radio station the first time doesn't mean that you will never get it.

If you are prone to generalization and sweeping conclusions whenever you have a setback, you need to start challenging your thought patterns.

"I had a bad day at work—but I am still good at what I do."

"We had an argument—but it does not mean we need to head for divorce court. We are still doing fundamentally fine."

"I overindulged today with chocolate and other stuff—but it does not mean I can't eat healthily. Tomorrow is another day."

Don't let yesterday's or today's disappointments stop you from succeeding tomorrow. Nobody knows what the future holds. If you were disappointed today, tell yourself, "It didn't happen today, but tomorrow is another day."

"It's My Fault"

Humankind is always trying to explain why things happen. If things don't work out, we want to find someone to blame. We blame others. Unhappy people often blame themselves.

If you have a tendency to blame yourself when things go wrong, closely examine the circumstances that led to the setback. Some of these may have had nothing to do with you. If you feel that you let yourself down at a job interview, try to think why. Maybe you weren't prepared enough, or maybe you had just been ill and were feeling tired. Is that your fault? Perhaps you just were not right for the job. That isn't your fault either. Perhaps you were right for the job but need to work on certain skills or gain more experience. Use the interview as a learning experience, and improve your skill base.

Never accept blame for things that are out of your control. Don't concentrate on your weaknesses; instead, turn your attention to your positive aspects. Fix your strengths firmly in your mind, and be ready to remember them, especially when things go wrong. Try to replace blaming thoughts with encouraging ones: "This didn't work out, but how was I to know this or that would happen?" It is impossible for you to be in control of all the factors that create a situation.

Fortune-Telling

Some things are likely to happen. The sun will rise in the morning and set in the evening. At night the moon and stars will come out. But there is no such thing as complete certainty. The world probably won't, but it could, end tomorrow!

When you start to see only the negative, you lose a sense of perspective. How do you know that things are going to go horribly wrong? If you are prone to negative thinking, it's likely that your predictions favor negative outcomes and that you treat these outcomes as facts. However, it is unlikely that everything will turn out unpleasant all the time.

If you keep searching the future for things you fear, start challenging that thinking now. If you think you know what other people are thinking, question that assumption. You can never know for sure what someone else is thinking; you are not a mind reader. It's more realistic to think that unpleasant things may or may not happen. Start allowing yourself the possibility that things may go right. Get rid of over-the-top pessimism.

If you have a tendency to think the worst of yourself and other people, take a deep breath and think about the evidence for and against your forecast. Start replacing negative assumptions with more realistic ones. "I keep thinking I'll never do well, but how can I tell what will happen in the future?" If you think you'll never amount to anything, repeatedly ask yourself, "How do I know?"

Ignoring the Positive

If you're far along in the downward spiral of negative thinking, you're likely to ignore anything positive that doesn't match your negative view. This stage is the bleakest of all. You reach a point where you can't see any meaning. You are tempted to give up. But life is full of disappointment and futility only if you think it is.

Challenge negative thoughts as much as you can by looking for facts to disprove them. You will start to learn that negative thinking not only makes you feel unhappy, it is also misleading and inaccurate.

Worry

Worry is the term we use to describe the state of mind that continually rehearses negative possibilities. Unless you find a way to manage worry, it tends to get worse and worse. Negative possibilities are magnified out of all proportion. Disturbing thoughts do seem to fly into our minds a lot, but we don't need to nurture them. Remember that you are in control of your thoughts. You may not be able to stop worrying from happening, but you can learn to cope with worry in a positive way.

The next time you start worrying try the following:

* Stop and recognize that you are worrying.
* Try to identify what is worrying you. If you don't know and just feel negative and anxious, see worry as a helpful warning sign that something in your life isn't working.
* Ask yourself, "Is there anything I can do to change the situation?" If there is, get on with it. If there isn't, change your attitude to the situation and find a substitute for the energy your worry is using up.
* If worry makes you tense, learn to relax your muscles.
* If worry is preventing you from making a decision, think of all the possible alternatives, weigh up the pros and cons, and take action. If mistakes occur, remind yourself that nobody can be 100 percent right all the time. Learn from the setback and try again.
* Most of the time worry is influenced by irrational thinking processes. Past events may be influencing the way you react to current situations, or faulty beliefs may cause problems. For instance, if you were rejected by your parents, you may feel that unless you win the approval of others you are worthless. Or you may feel that unless you act a certain way people won't like you.

It's time to start asking yourself questions again. Do you have any faulty or irrational beliefs that need to be replaced with more positive ones?

New Ways of Thinking

When you start becoming more familiar with your thinking biases, you can challenge them in the ways suggested previously. It might help to think about the worst thing that could happen. If you imagine that and prepare yourself mentally for the worst, anything else won't seem quite so bad. Start improving on the worst-case scenario, and think of other more positive outcomes. Think about your strengths as well as how others can help you cope.

High-quality thinking sounds simple, but it is a lot harder than you think. The key is practice. You are learning a new skill. You are learning to talk to yourself in a reassuring and supportive way. Your negative thoughts aren't used to being challenged. Keep practicing, and in time challenging them will become second nature. You will start recognizing when you are losing perspective, worrying too much, and seeing only the negative. One day constant put-downs and negative assessments of your ability won't seem so compelling anymore. They may even start to seem melodramatic, unrealistic, and slightly absurd.

Be a High-Quality Act

Go for quality in the chocolate that you eat and the kind of life you have. If you want your life to make a difference—no matter who you are or what you want to do—then you're first going to have to stand up for you. Most likely the person who is truly holding you back is not a member of your family, your boss, or the world in general. Who's holding you back is you. It's up to you to start challenging the way you think, feel, and behave.

Never forget one thing. You are the voice of your life, and it is through your voice, and your voice alone, that you will find the determination to make yourself a success. If you want to be a high-quality act, you can be. All you have to do is start thinking and behaving like one.

Pass the Chocolates

ABOUT CHOCOLATE: Perfect to give and receive, chocolate is made for sharing.

ABOUT LIFE: Give and receive in equal measure.

hocolate is the perfect gift to give and receive, and isn't giving and receiving what leading a happy, fulfilled life is really all about?

For the Love of Chocolate

Our abilities to give and receive are at the core of our capacity to create and experience true prosperity.

—Shakti Gawain, author

When you help someone out without expecting anything in return, you double your chances of happiness and good fortune. Blessings naturally return to you either in the good feelings you have about yourself or the good feelings others have about you. The trick, though, is to give of yourself without knowing how or even if happiness will come back to you, but trusting that if you are a kind, helpful person, it will return to you like a boomerang.

Say you take the time to give advice to a college student who wants to work in the same field as you. While you are chatting, the student learns that you enjoy music, because you mention a well-known orchestra. You don't see the student again, but six months later the student sends you advance information about a series of concerts taking place at her university. You decide to attend. When you arrive, you bump into an old friend you haven't seen for years. You swap phone numbers and agree to have dinner at your friend's house. You go to dinner and are introduced to someone who shares your passion for music, and it progresses from there. You fall in love and get married.

Happy people give unconditionally. The more they give, the happier they become because their efforts are selfless and without condition, which causes people to want to remember them or think well of them. Others may recommend you for an opportunity or work hard to repay you or go out of their way to give you suggestions and advice. Generosity breeds loyalty and respect and guarantees you a place in people's minds and hearts.

Sometimes, though, generosity's true reward isn't a favor returned but the warmth you feel after you have given. You feel good about yourself, and as we saw in Principle #1, feeling good about yourself is a vital ingredient for happiness. Research has proven that regular volunteer work increases life expectancy, decreases boredom, and creates an increased purpose in life. Studies show that volunteer workers are twice as likely to feel happy as nonvolunteers, so if you want to increase your chances of happiness, the best way is often to concentrate on the happiness of others.

Give from your heart, not your head, and never give under false pretenses in order to manipulate someone. Don't give when it's likely to cause you resentment, and never approach giving like a bookkeeper. The credit for your compassion may not show up for a long time, and it may not show up at all except in your heart. Give without asking—even sometimes without anyone else knowing.

Integrate Easy Giving Behaviors into Your Life

One kind word can warm three winter months.
—Japanese saying

Have you ever felt that everything is going wrong and then suddenly someone does something nice to you and turns your day around? Sometimes the smallest things—a hello, a kind note, a smile, a compliment, a surprise gift of chocolates, a hug—can make a huge difference. In relationships the little things are often the big things. Integrate easy giving and kindness into your life, and see how much better you feel.

If you love chocolate, giving is something that will come naturally to you. After all, chocolate is closely associated with giving and receiving. Here are some suggestions. Why not try adding other ideas of your own?

* Offer someone a compliment.
* Call on an elderly neighbor for five minutes a day to make sure he or she is okay.
* Drop off some flowers and chocolates to a nursing home with a request that it be given to someone who doesn't get many visitors.

* Let the person behind you in the supermarket with only a few items go ahead of you.
* At a restaurant, pile up your dishes in neat piles to make it easier for the waiter to clear.
* Call your mom or dad to say hello.
* Let a driver into traffic.
* Offer to babysit for a couple who can't get out much.
* Bring a box of chocolates with you to work, and leave it out for people to help themselves.

Life satisfaction has been shown to improve significantly with the level of altruistic activity. By helping others, we create positive bonds with others and think better of ourselves. In studies, those who had more opportunities to help felt much better about themselves than those who didn't have so many opportunities. Research has also shown that difficult circumstances in a person's life are a less strong predictor of their happiness or unhappiness than the amount of support available to them.

> Everybody forgets the basic thing: people are not going to love you unless you love them.
>
> —Pat Carroll, actress

Follow the golden rule, and treat others as you would want them to treat you. Think about what an offer of help means to someone else, not to you. If you ever have something nice to say, just say it. Don't wait until people are dead to send flowers. If you are concerned about feeling vulnerable, stop viewing relationships as a competition and see them more as a celebration. You don't win at relationships. You win by having relationships.

Think about what motivates you to give and what stops you giving. Think about what kind of giving activities bring you the most satisfaction and what kind of giving makes you feel burned out and resentful. Then, think about what you would like to do to increase the giving behavior that makes you feel good. Look for ways to do random acts of kindness every day. Try it for a week, and notice how good giving behavior makes you feel great.

Think Win-Win

A win-win attitude toward life says, "I can win, but so can you." It's the only attitude that can lead to happiness, and it's based on the principle of generosity, which is what Principle #6 is all about. But what is win-win? The best way to explain is to see what win-win is not. Win-win is not win-lose, lose-win, or lose-lose. These are all common but unhelpful attitudes to life.

Win-lose is an attitude toward life that says the chocolate box of success is only so big, and if you eat a piece there is less for me, so I'm going to make darn sure I get my share first. We've all been trained to think win-lose from an early age, so don't feel bad if you feel that winning is everything and get jealous when other people do better. It's a tough habit to break, especially when you begin to understand that winning doesn't equal happiness and if you've had to sacrifice friendship along the way, it's horribly lonely.

Lose-win is an attitude toward life that says, "I'm the nice guy, I'll do anything for the sake of peace." If you adopt this attitude to life, don't be surprised if other people take advantage and wipe their feet all over you. You'll also have to hide your true feelings, which isn't healthy. Lose-lose is a downward spiral. It's the attitude toward life that says, "If I'm unhappy and not doing well, then you are going down with me."

Win-win, however, is a belief that everyone can win. It's being nice and tough at the same time. I won't step on you, but I won't run around after you either. With a win-win attitude we care about other people and want them to succeed, but we care about ourselves too. Win-win is about abundance. It's the belief that there is plenty of success to go around. It's not about you or me; it's about us.

But how do you think win-win when your best friend gets the job you are after or your cousin gets spotted by a modeling agency and is destined for huge success? It all begins with you and how confident and secure you are in yourself. If you feel good about yourself, you won't feel threatened. Personal security is the foundation for thinking win-win (see Principle #1). Competition is healthy only when you compete against yourself or when it challenges and teaches you to become your best. Competition becomes unhealthy when you see it as a way to place yourself above others. Comparing yourself to others is equally poisonous.

Sometimes it may seem impossible to find a win-win solution, and someone may be so bent on competition that you can't move forward. When this happens and you can't find a solution, don't get sucked in; just call the game off.

Perhaps the best thing about win-win is the good feelings it brings on—and the true test of whether you are thinking win-win is how you feel. Thinking win-win will fill your heart with feelings of generosity and happiness.

The Power of Synergy

Synergy is the reward for thinking win-win. It is achieved when two or more people work together to create a better solution than they could have if they worked alone. Synergy is about celebrating differences, teamwork, open-mindedness, and finding new and better ways to work.

If you have ever been on a team, in a play, or in a band and things came together, you have felt it. Great teams are usually made up of different types of people, and each person brings his or her talents and contributes in a different way. The finest chocolate selections are made up of a different variety of chocolates, all bursting with tasty surprises.

Let's say that you are listening to a piece of music. All the voices and instruments may be singing and playing at once, but they aren't competing. Individually, the voices and instruments make different sounds, and they pause at different times. Yet blended together, they create a whole new sound. This is synergy. Synergy doesn't just happen; it is a process.

There are lots of successful independent people out there, but look closely and you will see that behind their success there is synergy. Take great sports figures. In order for them to compete at the level they do, a team of people is always backing them: the coach, the publicist, the masseur, the physiotherapist, the accountant, and so on. Each of these people focuses on what he or she is good at, and that in turn allows the sports player to be the best that he or she can possibly be. Would your favorite chocolate bar taste so sumptuous without a team of people to create and produce it?

To build synergy, you need to share your ideas and try to understand the ideas of others. After brainstorming for a while, the best idea will usually surface. But it takes a lot of maturity to get to synergy. You have to be willing to give and take, to work as part of a team. You need to listen, really listen, to other people's points of view and have the courage to express your own. You need to be willing to share. And you need to do all this with an open mind, which allows everyone's creative juices to flow.

Happy people are always creating synergy. While they focus

on what they are good at, they gather a team of people around them who have different strengths. And everyone shares in the end result, which is success, harmony, satisfaction, and, of course, happiness.

You Have Two Ears and One Mouth

A major roadblock on the way to win-win and synergy is a lack of generosity when it comes to listening to what other people are saying. The key to having power and influence with other people can be summed up in one sentence: listen before you talk. If you can learn this simple habit—to see things from another person's point of view—a whole new world of understanding will open to you.

It's the deepest need of the human heart to be understood, and the greatest gift you can give others is to respect and value them as they are—each a one-of-a-kind person who has something unique to say. The problem is that many of us don't know how to listen. We are often so busy preparing a response, judging, advising, paying attention only to what interests us, putting our own spin on things, or thinking of something else entirely that we completely miss the point.

To listen well, listen not just to the words a person says, but also to the tone of voice and the feelings reflected in his or her body language. Only 7 percent of communication is contained in the words we use. Take a genuine interest in the other person, and see things from that person's point of view without offering advice, judging, or probing. Allow the other to express their thoughts without constantly interrupting with your own. Conversations aren't competitions where one point of view wins. Since two people are coming from two different points of view, you can both be right. Restate or reflect back what is being said to you. This technique, called mirroring, will help you here. Mirroring the other person can be as simple as reflecting back what the person says using phrases such as "You feel that . . ." or "So what you are saying is . . ." or "I can see that you are feeling . . ." And don't be afraid of silence. A great deal can be said in times of silence: "I'm listening, I'm understanding, I'm here for you."

If you take the time to listen and understand, your chances of being listened to and understood are far better. When you need to give feedback, you can use your knowledge of that person to judge whether what you are going to say is in the other person's best interest. If you do need to make your feelings known, stay calm and say what you mean without casting blame. Use "I" messages instead of "you" messages. In other words, say, "I'm concerned about your health," or "I feel that we haven't been getting along lately." Talking about "you" is more threatening because it sounds as if you are blaming the other person: "You have been horrible to me." "You are not looking after yourself." Say what you mean but without causing offense.

Use questions that encourage communication, such as, "How did you feel about that?" or "What happened?" rather than questions requiring a yes or no answer.

Understanding another means stepping into that person's shoes and making room for the other's needs as well as your own. This will involve both giving and receiving on your part. It is well worth the effort it takes, for it will deepen your friendships and enrich your relationships.

Giving Too Much

You have probably heard the saying that only after you love yourself can you love someone else. The same applies to giving. Only after you know how to give to yourself can you give to others. Common sense and scientific research agree that until you have met your own physical and emotional needs, you can't muster sufficient resources for someone else. When you start to neglect yourself for the sake of other people, you simply can't be effective in helping them.

It is absolutely crucial that you learn how to take care of yourself so that you are at your best—physically, mentally, and emotionally. If you are exhausted and resentful because you are giving too much or have too much responsibility, you will block happiness from your life. Anger and negative thoughts will infiltrate your mind, or you may just be too tired to seize opportunities.

Be generous but not stupid. You don't want to be giving to people who are lazy or perpetuating their self-destruction. When successful people give assistance, their help isn't random. They think carefully about whom they are going to help. This isn't because they are expecting something in return. They simply know that their help will be more valued by, and therefore will be able to do more good for, people who appreciate and value their gifts.

Think about the ways you take care of and strengthen yourself. What makes you feel good? Do you give yourself regular breaks and time-outs? Do you stay connected to your friends and loved ones? How do you keep yourself healthy? Happy people know how important self-care is for their well-being, so they integrate it into their lives. Principle #7 is full of ways to be good to yourself, but there is one surefire way we'll explore first as it's all about sharing and making yourself vulnerable — love!

The Healing Power of Love

Relationships are all about giving and receiving, and Principle #6 urges you to cherish and value them. Research has shown that our health and happiness depend on the healing power of love, intimacy, and relationships.

The Food of Love

More than 1,400 years ago when cacao beans were used as money, chocolate was considered food of the gods, imparting wisdom and power to those who could afford it. The virile Aztec emperor Montezuma drank nothing but chocolate before visiting his harem. In 1659 chocolate was shipped to France, and it was proclaimed a miracle drug by local physicians. Rumors of its aphrodisiac qualities spread like wildfire. In the eighteenth century the legendary Casanova drank chocolate instead of champagne and said it was the elixir of love. (Drinking chocolate together has definite romantic and sexual overtones, but do make sure that it is good-quality chocolate and not a cheap substitute for cocoa.) The infamous Marquis de Sade was reputed to slip chocolate into desserts to loosen the libido of his guests. Monks were banned from drinking it in case their ardors got out of control, and an article written in the *Spectator* in 1712 warned readers about "meddling with chocolate, novels and the like which I look upon as very dangerous." But it was the Victorians who perfected the courtship rituals of heart-shaped boxes of chocolates presented on bended knee. Today chocolate continues to set the mood for love around the world, with chocolate lovers showering gifts of chocolate on those they care about.

Good relationships give you a sense of belonging and attachment. If you are not in a relationship, you can get the same effect from spending time with close friends or family or even your pet. Consider the following.

Loving thoughts and acts can make you feel better about yourself and boost your well-being. If you feel ill or down, try to be with someone who cares about you, or be extra caring toward yourself. When you get into a loving state of mind, your nervous system sends healthy, positive messages to your brain and immune system.

Perfect relationships don't exist, so enjoy the value of real relationships. For relationships to become really strong and intimate, the two of you need to learn to value each other's differences and get through the tough times. You also need to be able to make a commitment to each other. Having a commitment to another gives you a safe zone in which you can be vulnerable, and vulnerability makes greater intimacy possible.

Being touched boosts your well-being and immune system. Studies of patients with serious illnesses have shown that those who remain in close relationships stay healthier for longer. Babies who are hugged and held develop a lot earlier and faster than those who are not. So get a hug, a kiss, or a massage today. Make love more often.

Regular sex isn't just good exercise; research shows that sex helps to relieve insomnia and stress because it stimulates the release of feel-good hormones called endorphins. Sexual arousal also produces powerful hormones that encourage strong bonds with your partner. So if your sex life is losing its appeal, talk about it with your partner, spend time together, and bring some romance back into your relationship. Laugh together. When we share humor, we bring great intimacy to our relationships.

Hidden Meanings

Offering your lover or someone you hope will become your lover chocolates is one of the most romantic and seductive things you can do. For the past hundred years, giving chocolates to a loved one has been a sign of affection. A carefully selected and beautifully presented box of chocolates can say so much to the right person. But if you are going to give chocolate, do make sure it is good quality. The packaging for chocolate speaks volumes too. Chocolate looks best wrapped in gold rather than cheaper silver or blue, and it also looks good in black and red.

> There's no such thing as bad sex? Well, for me, there's no such thing as bad chocolate.
>
> — Woody Allen, actor and director

Heal your heart by sharing your feelings more. Write in your mood journal, talk to people you trust, or join a support group. Learn how to forgive. If you are carrying a grudge, make a point to drop it. Forgiving others frees you from the negative effects of anger on yourself.

Develop your spiritual life. Believing in a power greater than yourself allows you to feel part of and loved by a larger community. Prayer and meditation can give you a deeper level of interconnection with others. Love can be defined as anything that takes you out of the experience of being separate. And a powerful way to do that is to commune with God — or whatever name your give to that experience.

Chocolate and Sex

Heavenly, mellow, sensual, deep, dark, sumptuous, gratifying, potent, dense, creamy, seductive, rich, excessive, silky, smooth, luxurious, celestial. Chocolate is downfall, happiness, pleasure, love, ecstasy, fantasy. Chocolate makes us wicked, guilty, sinful, healthy, chic, happy.

—Elaine Sherman, *Madam Chocolate's Book of Divine Indulgences*

Chocolate is the perfect gift for lovers to give and receive. But why is chocolate so sexy? Many years ago it was marketed as a health product, with mothers feeding it to their children to give them energy and stamina, but these days chocolate is linked to sex. It's easy to see why.

Chocolate is an aphrodisiac in that it contains chemicals that create a sense of excitement and well-being, conducive to love-making. Your hormones are affected by these chemicals, and sexual stimuli pass to a part of the brain called "the pleasure center." This sends signals to your pelvic region, and your libido soars.

It isn't just the chemical content that makes chocolate sexy. Chocolate is pretty much like sex in many ways. It has to be unwrapped, it gives us a lift, it is consumed with passion, and it can be soft, melting, and sensual. It's versatile too. You can have your chocolate alone or share it with your lover. You can eat it quickly or take it nice and slow. Chocolate is also sexy because it makes you feel indulgent and naughty. It's a way of treating yourself that is both enjoyable and satisfying to all the senses.

Chocolate and Sex: What More Could Your Body Want?

Recent surveys suggest that as many as one in four women prefer chocolate to sex. So is chocolate better than sex? You decide, but here are some fun reasons to consider, and I'm sure you can think of lots more:

❖ You can always get chocolate.
❖ You can eat chocolate in public.
❖ You can have as many types of chocolate as you like without people saying you are easy.
❖ You can go right to sleep after chocolate.
❖ You always feel like having chocolate.
❖ Chocolate isn't scared of the word *commitment*.

Allow Others to Give to You

Some people find it hard to allow lovers or friends or anyone to give to them. They may hold the misguided belief that receiving puts them in a vulnerable position. It is easier to be in the power position of giver, creating indebtedness rather than feeling indebted. It is easy to put up a wall and pretend to be self-sufficient. That way you don't have to know that you have needs or face the possibility that someone will disappoint you. Relying on other people can make you feel out of control.

But Principle #6 isn't just about giving, it's about giving and receiving in equal measure. To increase your chances of happiness, you need to let others give to you. I bet that you wouldn't have a problem accepting a gift of chocolates, so why not accept a helping hand or a compliment when it is given? Why not let your partner take the initiative in bed? Remember, it isn't always about you. Other people have just as much need to give and offer love as you do. Why not let other people feel good about themselves by receiving and being grateful for help and love when it is offered to you?

If you have problems with receiving, ask yourself why and how you are blocking good things from happening to you. What is threatening to you about receiving? What can you do today to open yourself more to receiving love and help from other people?

The universe rewards an open hand and heart, not a closed fist. Open yourself up to giving and receiving, and watch your life become lighter, easier, and brighter. Why base your life on fear and insecurity when it doesn't have to be that way? There's an old saying about two men looking out through a prison gate. One saw mud, and the other saw stars. Why look at the mud when you can look at the stars?

Principle #6 shows you that happiness and love are always knocking on the door, but they won't come to you unless you open the door and are willing to let them in.

Chocolate Heaven

~

ABOUT CHOCOLATE: Chocolate is the Prozac of candy. Eating it makes you feel good.

ABOUT LIFE: Only you can heal your life.

hocolate can give you a quick boost when you need it, but the fix is temporary. Principle #7 is all about finding permanent ways to lift yourself up.

> After eating chocolate you feel godlike, as though
> you can conquer enemies, lead armies, entice lovers.
> — Emily Lauchetti, American pastry chef

Healing Your Life

When you feel good about yourself, your mind, body, emotions, and spirit are balanced. If you aren't feeling at your best, ask yourself:

Have I taken care of myself physically today?
How much mental activity have I had today?
Have I been in touch with my feelings today?
Have I taken some time out today?

When we feel balanced in the four interrelated aspects of ourselves—the physical, the emotional, the mental, and the spiritual—we feel happy and fulfilled. If for some reason we are out of balance, we are not at ease with ourselves and our lives. It's up to each of us to discover where the balance lies and then find ways to recreate it.

Why is balance so important? Because what you do in one aspect of your life will affect the other three. Think about it. It's hard to be friendly (heart), alert (mind), and in tune with yourself (soul) when you feel ill (body). To perform at your peak, you need to strive for balance in all four areas.

If you are not balanced and have been neglecting your health and well-being, dealing with life is rather like trying to cut a tree with a blunt ax. But if you take the time to sharpen the ax, progress will be much quicker.

To heal means to make whole. Every time we have a problem, be it physical, emotional, spiritual, or mental, we are being shown a place where we need to heal ourselves. Chocolate can give you a temporary boost when you feel low, but it's not a long-term solution for unhappiness. It's a bit like sticking a Band-Aid over an injury that needs a full bandage. It will help, but not enough to stop the bleeding. You need something stronger and larger.

The only way to find lasting contentment is to understand that ultimately your own healing rests with you. Only you know what you need for your body, mind, heart, and soul—only you can choose to create health and well-being in your life. The tips that follow for balancing yourself suggest ways for you to take charge of your own healing so that you feel happy and healthy in all areas of your life.

Your Body

We are what we eat. If we put the wrong kind of gas in the car, it won't run smoothly. The same applies to us. If we eat things that are unsuitable for us, we will not feel our best, look our best, or perform our best. Be aware of what you are putting into your body. Know when to stop when you have had enough. Make sure you eat lots of vegetables and fruits and an adequate amount of protein. Eat high-fiber carbohydrates, and avoid sugar, alcohol, caffeine, and excessive fats. Drink lots of water to clear out toxins. If you have been eating things without thought, then try breaking the habit for just one day to demonstrate that you do have the strength to take in the best nutrients for your body. Then try for two days, and so on, until eating well becomes a habit that increases your feelings of general well-being.

How to Include Chocolate in a Healthy, Balanced Diet

As we saw in Principles #3 and #4, chocolate can enhance our health as long as we eat it in moderation. Try some of these review tips:

Eat chocolate with or soon after a meal when you are less tempted to overeat and pile on the extra calories.

Buy small bars rather than family boxes or bars.

Dip fresh fruit in chocolate-flavored syrup.

Choose bars that contain chocolate chips or chocolate chunks. They can satisfy the urge with fewer calories.

Try to balance your chocolate consumption with regular exercise.

Go for high-quality dark chocolate, which is higher in stearic acids and antioxidants than milk chocolate.

Eat small servings several times a week to avoid bingeing when you feel stressed or depressed.

Eat chocolate slowly; don't gulp it down. Let chocolate sit in your mouth for a few seconds to release its primary aromas; then chew it a few times to release its secondary aromas. Next, let it rest lightly against the roof of your mouth so you experience the full range of flavors and texture. Finally enjoy its lingering taste before you devour the next piece.

Pay attention to your feelings. Are you reaching for too much chocolate because you feel sad, alone, unhappy, angry, or afraid? Reread the section on eating for comfort. Is there a nonchocolate solution?

Pay attention to your nutrient and calorie intake. A 50-gram bar of plain chocolate contains 255 calories, 14 g fat, 17 mg calcium, 2.2 mg iron, 45 mg magnesium. A

50-gram bar of milk chocolate contains 260 calories, 15 g fat, 110 mg calcium, 0.7 mg iron, 25 mg magnesium. A 50-gram bar of white chocolate contains 265 calories, 15 g fat, 135 mg calcium, trace elements of iron, and 13 mg magnesium.

People who exercise—whether an intense workout or just a regular long walk—feel healthier and better about themselves and enjoy their lives more. Regular exercise, including brisk walking, directly increases happiness and can indirectly make a dramatic contribution to improving self-image. Research on physical activity finds that exercise increases self-confidence. So why do so many of us avoid it?

We often make unrealistic promises in the keep-fit department, and then we feel bad about ourselves when we can't live up to them. So, keep your goals realistic. Just begin with three 10-minute sessions each week. If you are unused to exercise, set small goals, such as walking short distances instead of driving, taking the stairs instead of the elevator. Small achievements will develop your inclination and motivation to increase your exercise, and once you start to feel better and enjoy the benefits, there will be no stopping you.

Get a good night's sleep. A full night's rest provides fuel for the next day, making you work better and feel more comfortable when the day is over. Studies show that having good-quality and and an adequate quantity of sleep contributes to health, well-being, and a positive outlook. For those who sleep less than eight hours, every hour of sleep results in an 8 percent less positive feeling about their day. Too much sleep, say more than twelve hours, can also be unhelpful.

Lack of good-quality sleep is one of the biggest causes of low self-esteem. Don't panic if you aren't getting eight hours of sleep every night. Everyone has different sleep needs. The best indicator of sleep need is how you feel during the day. Are you alert, energetic, and able to concentrate? If you feel exhausted, irritable, and as if you are about to doze all the time, you are not getting enough sleep. Here are a few suggestions to help you sleep better: Try to establish regular waking and sleeping times so that you set up a sleeping pattern. Make sure that your bedroom is comfortable and quiet. Avoid heavy meals, exercise, and caffeine at least two hours before you go to sleep. Relax as much as you can before you go to bed. Take a warm bath or listen to some soothing music. Have a milky hot chocolate before you go to bed.

Your Mind

Finding and developing a hobby or talent or special interest is one of the most important things you can do to recreate balance in your life. There are all kinds of things you may be good at. You may have a talent for reading, writing, or speaking. You may have a good memory or a gift for creativity or helping others. You may have organizational, music, or leadership skills. It doesn't matter where your interests lie. When you do something you like, it is a form of self-expression. It's fun, it sharpens your mind, and it builds your self-esteem.

Look for something new. Education doesn't stop when you leave school. Keep learning and discovering all the time. Looking for something new encourages your imagination and interest. Children have a natural interest in the world around them. Unfortunately, as we get older, we often lose this interest in life, and this can lead to fatigue and boredom. An adventurous spirit encourages creativity, excitement, and good feelings about yourself. When you do something new, you always feel more energetic, and you learn something new about yourself. Go to a concert to listen to some music you don't normally listen to, sign up for an evening class, learn a new language, visit a place where you have never been, vary your routine. The possibilities are endless.

Good smells awaken the senses and the brain and at a subconscious level remind us of good things. Research shows that pleasant smells evoke surprise and happiness, while unpleasant smells trigger disgust and unhappy reactions. Here's a quick way to feel good about yourself: air out your house and add some fragrant flowers. Make your home smell nice, and you will feel the benefits.

Your Heart

Reconnect with your feelings: our feelings are very important, but we often don't know what we are feeling. If you aren't in touch with your feelings, you can't be true to yourself, and your self-esteem will be low. Give yourself feeling checks throughout the day, Stop and ask yourself, "What am I feeling?" "Why does this make me feel a certain way?" "Does this feel good?" "Does this feel bad?" This will help you become more aware of your feelings and help you recognize your needs.

And when everything seems to be going crazy or you do something really stupid, keep your heart healthy and strong by laughing. Sometimes life sucks and there is nothing you can do about it, so you may as well laugh.

> True happiness is of a retired nature and an enemy
> to pomp and noise; it arises, in the first place,
> from the enjoyment of one's self and, in the next,
> from the friendship and conversation of a few
> select companions.
>
> —Joseph Addison,
> English politician and writer (1642–1719)

Cultivate friendships. As discussed in Principle # 6, if you want to know if people are happy, don't ask them about how much money they have in the bank. Ask them about their relationships. Researchers have identified the core factors in a happy life. The primary components are closeness of friends and family and relationships with coworkers and neighbors. Together these features explain about 70 percent of personal happiness.

Take advantage of opportunities to make friends. We all need to feel that we are part of something bigger, that we care about others, and that others care about us in return. According to one study, if you feel close to other people, you are four times more likely to feel good about yourself than if you do not feel close to anyone. So, place a high value on your friendships, keep your promises, be loyal, be supportive, be kind, listen to what your friends have to say, apologize if you make a mistake, and set out clear expectations. Tell it like it is, and be honest about who you are and what others can expect of you.

It isn't only friendships of a human kind that can help us feel good about ourselves. Research shows that interaction with animals supplies us with both immediate joy and long-term positive feelings and contributes strongly to our happiness. Those with a loved pet are more likely to feel satisfied than those without.

Enjoy What You Have

The last two miles of the hill were terrible and I said, "Japhy there's one thing I would like right now more than anything in the world more than anything I have ever wanted in my life." Cold dusk winds were blowing, we hurried bent with our backs on the endless trail. "What?" "A nice big Hershey bar or even a little one. For some reason or other, a Hershey bar would save my soul right now."

—Jack Kerouac, *Dharma Bums*

Too often when we think about our lives, we think about what we don't have, but happy people know the importance of appreciating what they do have in life. Imagine that you are ninety-five years old and you are looking back at your life now. What are you taking for granted? Your health, your friends, your family, your freedom? Appreciate what you have, and focus on what is good about your life. Gratitude and an optimistic attitude are prerequisites for a happy life. Squeeze them out of your present circumstances as hard as you can.

Your Soul

I have discovered that all man's unhappiness
derives from only one source—not being able to sit
quietly in a room.

—Blaise Pascal, French philosopher,
mathematician, and physicist

When we forget to pay attention to our spirits, we become
nervous, stressed, and afraid. We are all creatures of the earth,
and the world will offer us support and calm if we take the
time to connect with it.

Feeling low is often the result of trying too hard to keep up
with the pressures of modern life and neglecting our souls.
Take a natural break to enjoy the simple pleasures and restore
your self-esteem. One of the most effective ways to calm your
mind is to get in touch with nature. Plan to escape the town
or city, even if for only a few hours a week. If this isn't possible, take a walk in the park. Take time to appreciate the won-
ders of nature, the color of the sky, the green of the grass, the
song of the birds. Slow down for a while and enjoy the peace
and quiet. It is surprising how quickly you can restore yourself
in these ways.

To lead a balanced life with inner strength, we need to be
able to stop doing and sometimes just be. Just being releases

tension and increases our self-awareness. If you find it hard to be, inner peace will elude you. Spend a few minutes each day in total silence. Turn off the TV or radio. Don't read a book or do anything. This will be difficult at first, so don't sit for too long. As you get used to it, you will be able to do it for longer and be able to balance your being with your doing.

Don't be afraid of being by yourself. Celebrate your aloneness. No one else can know you as well as you do. Don't think of this as scary. Would you really want anyone to know everything about you? The idea of being alone carries with it a wonderful quality of freedom from expectations and guilt. Frightening or freeing—your aloneness can be one or the other. Choose freedom. Choose to celebrate your aloneness and the fact that you are absolutely individual and special.

Handling Stress

One of the biggest threats to our sense of balance and well-being is stress. Stress often occurs when there is some kind of imbalance in your life. The first step is to recognize the source of the stress. Stand back and take a look at your life. Is your job too demanding? Are you unhappy in your relationship? Once you identify what is causing tension, you can take action to ease the tension and restore balance in your life. If this isn't possible—say you have a busy job and a busy family life and need to juggle both or you have an elderly relative to take care of—you need to find new ways to manage stress. And one of the best ways is to learn how to relax. We talked about relaxing in Principle #4, and there we used it to manage anxiety. Now we're using it for basic health maintenance.

Chill Out

Relaxation is the time when you recharge your batteries and focus on what makes you feel good. It has been scientifically proven that at least 80 percent of all illnesses can be controlled through relaxation. We need about thirty minutes of proper relaxation a day to balance our blood pressure, regulate our pulse, and moderate any other symptoms of stress.

Relaxation involves more than just sitting down with your feet up. You need to be able to relax your body and your mind at the same time—and by using simple techniques this is quite easy to achieve. Although it will certainly be beneficial to set aside specific times for deep relaxation each day, there is much to be said for relaxing a few moments at any time. This will help you return to your tasks fresh and alert and will prevent stress from building up.

There are many ways to relax, and some that work well for you may not work well for others. Try several techniques and find what works for you. The top five relaxation techniques are deep breathing (see below), meditation, massage, taking a long, soothing bath, and listening to music or a relaxation tape.

It is important to learn how to relax in response to bodily tension. You may be able to do this by watching a movie or reading a book or listening to music or playing an instrument, but if you can't relax, you need to learn how to take time out. One way to do this is to relax your whole body slowly, muscle by muscle. Start by dropping your shoulders, relaxing the muscles in your body and in your face—it's amazing how many of us frown without knowing it—breathing deeply, and gently relaxing. Many tapes on the market can help you through the process.

Just Say Omm!

Techniques such as meditation can also have astonishing results if you feel stressed. Meditation is one of the simplest ways to relax and allow stress to flow away naturally. It not only leads to mental peace and serenity, it also tunes your mind so that it functions more efficiently.

Meditation is not complicated—it involves sitting silently and focusing on one object or sound and allowing the mind to empty of all extraneous thoughts so that both body and mind relax completely. However, like many such simple-sounding techniques, this can be difficult to achieve without a great deal of practice. At first, the constant activity of your mind will be difficult to slow down, and stray thoughts will constantly break through and interrupt your concentration. However, your efforts will improve with practice, so try to set aside a specific time each day. It does not have to be a long period—better a short time that you can manage on a regular basis than a longer period that is difficult to fit into your schedule. As you begin to feel the benefits, you will be motivated to find more time.

Try this simple routine either first thing in the morning or just before you go to bed: Choose a focus word or phrase—for example, *peace* or *happy* or *chocolate*. Sit quietly, and relax your body by tensing and then relaxing your muscles and breathing deeply. Say the focus word every time you exhale. If you lose concentration, simply return your thoughts to the word. Try this for just five minutes at first, and then gradually increase the amount of time. Do the routine at least once a day.

Don't expect relaxation or meditation to be easy. If you are used to feeling tense, relaxing is a skill that has to be practiced. If you feel uncomfortable at first, don't worry; just accept that it will take time. Make sure that you are breathing deeply and not practicing when you are hungry, full, or overtired. Make your environment conducive to relaxation. If you fall asleep easily, you might want to avoid lying down. Expect your practice to be interrupted by worrying thoughts. The best way to deal with them is not to dwell on them. Just accept that they will drift into your mind from time to time, and then refocus on your relaxation.

If you don't feel the benefit right away, don't give up or try too hard. Just let the sensation of relaxation happen. Correct breathing will help.

Sweet Breathing

Chocolate is not only pleasant of taste but it's also a veritable balm of the mouth, for the maintaining of all glands and humors in a good state of health. This it is, that all who drink it possess a sweet breath.

—Stephani Blancardi, Italian physician (1650–1702)

The way we breathe is important. Deep, slow breathing through your nose rather than your mouth while allowing your abdomen to move can calm both your body and your mind and help you cope with stress. Try a simple yoga breathing exercise: Breathe in slowly through your nose while counting to five, hold your breath for a count of five, breathe out slowly through your nose for a count of five, wait a count of five, and repeat as often as you like. Concentrating on breathing and counting can be wonderfully calming for your mind, while the regular breathing will calm your body.

When you are stressed, you may hyperventilate or breathe rapidly. This rapid breathing is a natural response to stress or exertion. It uses the upper part of the lungs and results in too much oxygen intake. Rapid breathing isn't a problem if it is short term, but if it becomes habitual, it results in too much oxygen being taken into your bloodstream, upsetting the balance of oxygen and carbon dioxide. Unpleasant physical symptoms can result, such as tingling in your hands or face, muscle cramps, dizziness, fatigue, and aches and pains. These symptoms can be quite alarming, and they can trigger another cycle of stress.

It is easy to learn how to breathe correctly when you are anxious. Avoid breathing from your upper chest, and avoid gulping or gasping. When you first try to breathe correctly, you might want to lie down to feel the difference between deep breathing and shallow breathing.

First exhale as much as you can, then inhale gently and evenly through your nose, filling your lungs completely so that your abdominal muscles move outward. Finally, exhale slowly and fully. Repeat this, trying to get a rhythm going. You might want to aim to take ten breaths a minute. If you are not getting enough air, return to a breathing that is normal for you. Then try increasing the length of one breath, breathing out fully, then in fully, then out again. If that breath felt comfortable, try another one. To get a rhythm going, it's important not to try hard but to cooperate as easily as you can with your breathing muscles.

Alternate nostril breathing balances the left and right sides of your brain, relaxes the nervous system, and calms the body and mind. Sit straight but relaxed with one hand to your face so you can use the thumb to block one nostril and a finger to block the other. Close your left nostril and breathe in through the right, counting to three. Now, close your right nostril, exhale through the left nostril, and count to six. Breathe in again through your left nostril, and repeat alternately ten times.

It is important to practice correct breathing every time you feel stressed. As you practice, you will find that it gets easier and easier to breathe deeply instead of rapidly.

Imagine, Imagine, Imagine

Another stress-busting technique is creative visualization. This involves seeing events clearly in your imagination as you would like them to be. If you do this over and over, your mind eventually will accept it as reality. The problem with many of us is that we are constantly visualizing successfully—but using negative images instead of positive ones. Filling your mind with thoughts of failure will inevitably cause you to fail.

Creative visualization is one of the simplest ways to banish worry and stress. The key to making visualization work is to develop a positive scenario for any event that is worrying you and to continually rehearse it in your mind. As you keep repeating these positive thoughts, you will face stressful situations in a positive way, and this will greatly reduce your anxiety. As you reprogram your mind, it will begin to replace worry and negative thoughts with optimism and positive thoughts. Try the following:

* If you feel angry, upset, or stressed, imagine your bad feelings growing wings, and then watch them fly away.
* If you feel stressed, imagine walking along a beautiful beach in the sunshine. Feel the sand between your toes.
* If you are feeling pain, visualize what shape and color the pain is and then imagine it dissolving away.
* If you have problems fantasizing scenarios, use happy memories from your past. Happy thoughts lift your emotions and alter the body's chemistry in a positive way.

Use visualization to find a place of peace, to change the way you react to the world, find inner security, and create a secure future.

Massage

Just as we know the power of the mind to relax the body, we also know the power of the body to relax and quiet the mind. One of the most powerful physical ways to relax is by using various forms of massage. As well as relaxing the muscles, a full massage also boosts the lymph and blood circulation, the nervous system, and the body's flow of energy. Studies have shown that massage doesn't just relax your muscles; it gives you a much-needed time-out in which you can revel in a feeling of being cared for.

Massage is one of the oldest and simplest medical treatments, although in the West it has only recently become accepted for its wider health benefits. It can be stimulating or soothing and can relieve tension and induce a sense of well-being. Essentially, massage is an extension of something we often do automatically—we rub painful areas and stroke distressed children to soothe them. Even stroking a household pet is a form of massage, which has been proven to lower blood pressure and have a relaxing effect on both you and the pet. There are several different massage techniques, but most are fairly easy to learn. The simplest forms, such as stroking, kneading, circling, heel-of-hand pushing, thumb rolling, and fingertip pushing, relax the muscles, ligaments, and tendons to relieve tension. More complicated techniques, such as shiatsu and reflexology, can be used to unblock energy paths and realign the entire body.

Creative visualization, massage, and deep breathing can be beneficial, but so can a good night's sleep, regular exercise, healthy eating, yoga, soaking in a hot tub, listening to your favorite music, chatting with friends, cultivating outside interests and diversions from your usual routine, or putting your feet up and savoring every bite of your favorite chocolate bar. There are so many wonderful ways to relax. Many of us think of relaxation as time we can't afford to lose. Rather than thinking of it as time lost, think of it as time gained. When you return to your routine, you will feel refreshed and energized, and better able to cope.

Smile and the World Smiles with You

But perhaps the best way of all to reduce stress is the simplest—enjoy your life more. The positive emotions associated with laughter decrease stress hormones and increase the number of immune system cells. Think about all the things you really enjoy doing, and then try to work as many as possible of them into your life every day.

The chocolate principles have shown you what research is now proving—that pleasure does the immune system good. The more fun you have, the more gracefully you will age and the healthier you will feel. When we are happy, positive hormone and enzyme levels are elevated and our blood pressure is normal. Even smiling can send impulses along the pleasure pathways to make you feel good. And besides, wrinkles from smiling are far more attractive than harsh frown lines.

Many studies have linked happiness to longevity and demonstrated that there are considerable health benefits in happiness and humor. It is important not only to find pleasure in your daily routine but also to keep planning pleasurable activities in the future. And don't forget the chocoholic's mantra: Chocolate makes everyone smile—even bankers!

The Prozac of Candy

Chocolate acts on chemicals in our brains called neurotransmitters, releasing serotonin and endorphins, which make us feel good. And our level of phenylethylalmine also increases, inducing feelings of pleasure — the same things we feel when we fall in love. Chocolate's high levels of magnesium also contribute to the euphoria we get when we eat it.

Many of us take ourselves far too seriously. Remember how nervous and unsure you felt on your first date? Perhaps now you can look back with a smile. Have you ever thought that a few years from now you might look back and feel the same about what is worrying you now?

Children laugh hundreds of times a day. Having fun and playing don't need to stop just because you aren't a child anymore. Research shows that playing imaginative games can benefit concentration, coordination, attention span, and general health and well-being. But it doesn't really matter what the experts say, it's common sense. If you don't have laughter and fun in your life, are you really living?

Love Yourself to Heal Your Life

Feeling balanced 100 percent of the time isn't going to be possible. There will always be times when we feel as if we are off course, but this doesn't matter. Life's a journey, after all, and the more you discover along the way, the more exciting and fulfilling it is. The important thing is to keep hoping and looking for ways to recreate balance and good feelings about yourself. Chocolate is one surefire way to lift yourself up, but don't limit yourself to one; there are millions of others. Go on, try some of them out. You know you want to!

Principle #7 ends where we began with Principle #1. It reminds you that you can't make any progress with your life until you believe that you deserve to be loved. The better you feel about yourself, the more balanced your life will be and the more whole you will feel. So love and appreciate yourself to heal your life. Remind yourself that you are a valuable and good person who deserves to feel happy. You were born with all that you need to succeed. You don't need to look elsewhere. The power and light are within you and always will be with you.

The more you lift yourself up with loving and positive thoughts and take control of your life with a sense of direction and hope, the lighter, brighter, healthier, and happier your life will be. You'll feel balanced and whole as a person, and nothing, not even chocolate—although sometimes it comes very, very close—can fill you with such indescribable pleasure.

Chocolate 'Round the World

> The divine drink which builds up resistance and fights fatigue. A cup of this precious drink permits a man to walk for a whole day without food.
>
> —Hernán Cortés, Spanish explorer (1485–1547)

Chocolate wasn't always eaten as a sweet confection. For centuries it was only used for drinking. Chocolate has changed a great deal, and you wouldn't recognize the dark and bitter brew the ancient Aztecs knew as chocolate.

The Aztecs used chocolate as a drink rather than a food, flavoring it with various spices, including vanilla and chili pepper. They called this drink *xocoatl*, and it was served cold and tasted bittersweet. It was an important part of the Mayan and Aztec cultures over three thousand years ago. In 1519 Hernán Cortés was offered xocoatl at the court of Emperor Montezuma II (1502–1520), the last Aztec ruler of Mexico. Montezuma was perhaps the world's first chocoholic, because he was said to have consumed fifty jars of xocoatl a day, and he made sure that the members of his royal household were given two thousand jars a day.

The Food of the Gods

The Aztecs believed that cacao had a divine origin, the cacao tree being a metaphorical bridge between earth and heaven. Therefore, drinking a chocolate beverage was thought to confer godly qualities, such as wisdom and knowledge, on the individual. Cacao beans and chocolate were used in various religious ceremonies, chocolate, for example, being drunk during marriage ceremonies.

Other ancient cultures also used cacao butter in their religious ceremonies, and time and time again we come across the symbolism or properties of chocolate as a food to connect the individual to the divine. It was often rubbed into the feet to promote a trancelike state, as it was thought it could help a person journey symbolically to the divine realms.

The Spaniard Hernán Cortés took Montezuma prisoner (he

later died in custody) and brought xocoatl back to Spain, where it was sweetened and vanilla and cinnamon added instead of chili powder. Chocolate remained exclusive to the Spanish for a good hundred years until it began to be used in Italy, France, and other parts of Europe. It still remained a luxury item only the rich could afford because of the high import duties on cacao beans. In France chocolate was also sold for its medicinal properties and was used to treat fevers, coughs, chest and stomach pains, and as an aid to put on weight.

It's a Chocolate, Chocolate World

Gradually chocolate houses began to spring up all over Europe as meeting places for the fashionable and the learned. The chocolate drink that enjoyed such popularity then was made from a crumbly, coarse paste that had a high fat content. But there was still no eating chocolate for chocoholics until solid chocolate became popular about two centuries later. In 1849 the first truly commercial eating chocolate appeared at a trade fair in Birmingham, England. The bars were made by a company called Fry, which added sugar and chocolate liquor to the cocoa butter. Fry was followed by Cadbury.

The emergence of chocolate in America dates back to the eighteenth century, when America started processing cocoa beans brought back from voyages to the West Indies. In 1900 the very first Hershey bars began to appear in many American stores, and chocolate shops soon sprang up in every town. In fact, it wasn't until chocolate appeared in the United States that people began spelling and pronouncing it the way we do today, as "chocolate."

Turning Trees into Chocolate

The cacao tree is a remarkable and unique plant that grows to a height of forty feet in the Amazon forests, and its seeds are used to produce chocolate. The seeds of the cacao are commonly called beans, and they are contained in the pods, or fruit, of the tree. Cacao trees are unusual in that their fruit and flowers grow out of the trunk and the lower branches of the tree. The pods grow to a size of about 8 inches by 2¾ inches (20 cm by 7 cm), and each pod contains twenty to forty beans.

Over time the word *cacao* became interchangeable with *cocoa*, which is an Anglicization of the word. *Cocoa* now tends to refer to the fat-free powder produced from cacao paste. Once harvested, the cocoa beans are fermented, roasted, and shelled. The meat of the bean is ground to yield a powder, from which cocoa butter and cocoa liquor are extracted. Chocolate makers call this residue cocoa mass. The mass is then reblended with the cocoa butter and cocoa liquor to make the different types of chocolate.

Conching is the next step in the process. A conch is a container filled with refined, blended chocolate mass heated to a liquid consistency. The amount of conching time determines the smoothness and quality of the chocolate. Conching can take up to one week for high-quality chocolates, while for cheaper chocolates it may only take a few hours. The final process is called tempering. The chocolate is cooled down and rewarmed in stages. Chocolate is sold as a liquid or in blocks before the final manufacturing process.

> The superiority of chocolate both for health and nourishment will soon give it the same preference over tea and coffee in America which it has in Spain.
>
> —Thomas Jefferson, U.S. president

Richard Cadbury (the founder of England's Cadbury chocolate company) introduced a terrific moneymaking tradition by creating the first Valentine's Day candy box in 1868. Robert Stroehecker is the "father" of the first chocolate Easter bunny—

yet another successful holiday advertising icon, which first appeared in 1890. The United States Armed Forces also helped make chocolate a popular treat. During both World Wars, the rations of U.S. soldiers included this sweet for extra energy, and today, army D-rations still include four ounces of chocolate. Estimates suggest that the average person in the United States eats twelve to fourteen pounds of chocolate each year!

Chocolate: The Last Word on Our Consuming Passion

Today our craving for chocolate outstrips that for any other food in the West. There is no escaping the fact that chocolate is the world's favorite treat, but as the chocolate principles show us, chocolate is far more than a food; it's a fundamental part of our lives. Happiness, pleasure, giving, receiving, love, ecstasy, fantasy—with just a hint of danger. It's all right there, tempting us with the sweet smell of success.

I hope that through the principles in this book you have come to know more about your real self and the passion, love, and gifts that you have to offer. Be as willing to unwrap those gifts as you are to unwrap a box of chocolates. Your family, friends, and colleagues will benefit. And you will benefit in ways that you may not even be able to imagine—yet.

Appendix

Guilt-Free Indulgence

Here are some decadent chocolate treats you shouldn't even *try* to resist. *This is a guilt-free zone.* If cooking isn't your thing or you just haven't got the time, no worries—all the chocolates, cakes, and desserts below can be found at your local supermarket and bakery.

When cooking with chocolate, semisweet chocolate is the best to use because it gives a good strong flavor. However, quality varies considerably according to the proportion of cocoa solids listed in the ingredients. The higher the percentage of cocoa solids, the better the chocolate. It should contain a minimum of 34 percent, and the best contains 60 percent or more.

Milk chocolate is not satisfactory for use in cooking, but if it is melted, you can fill a pastry bag and pipe it onto semisweet chocolate for a decorative effect. White chocolate isn't normally used for cooking either, but its creamy texture means that it can sometimes be used in cold desserts. Baking chocolate is best reserved for baked goods. Couverture, confectionery coatings, and unsweetened and sweetened cocoa powder generally are not suitable for use in uncooked dishes but are terrific for achieving flavor when baking.

When melting chocolate, break it into small pieces and then try one of these methods:

* Choose a heat-proof bowl, and set it over a pan of simmering water. The bowl should not touch the water. Heat gently until the chocolate is melted, stirring occasionally.
* Put the broken chocolate into a microwavable bowl and microwave on low. Check the chocolate after one minute; then continue microwaving in small bursts until it starts to look shiny. Take it out of the microwave and stir until melted.

Note: For all recipes below I'm working on the assumption that one cup = approximately 8 ounces.

Gorgeous Gooey Gateau

Take your time.

This deeply delicious cake is rich, moist, and oozing with flavor.

13 ounces good-quality plain chocolate
½ cup milk
1 stick plus 1 tablespoon unsalted butter
1 tablespoon dark muscovado sugar
6 medium eggs
1 cup self-raising flour, sifted
⅓ cup ground almonds
For the icing:
10 ounces plain chocolate
3 tablespoons unsalted butter

Preheat oven to 350°F. Grease and line two 8-inch round cake pans. Melt chocolate with the milk in a dish over a pan of simmering water. Stir until smooth. Cool slightly.

Cream together butter and sugar in a bowl until light and fluffy; then gradually beat in eggs, adding a little flour if the mixture begins to curdle. Stir in the melted chocolate.

Lightly fold in remaining flour and then the ground almonds until evenly combined. Turn the mixture into prepared pans, and level the surfaces. Bake for 25 minutes until cakes are firm on the top and a skewer when inserted comes out clean. Cool 5 minutes before removing from pans.

Make the icing: Melt chocolate and butter over a pan of simmering water until the mixture becomes smooth and velvety. Cool 5 minutes.

Spread some icing between the cake layers, and sandwich together. Use a palette knife to coat the top and the sides with the rest.

Serves 12.

The Best Brownies in the World
Heaven on earth!

1½ **cups sugar**
1½ **sticks butter**
3 **ounces (3 squares) baking chocolate**
3 **beaten eggs**
½ **teaspoon vanilla**
½ **cup all-purpose flour**
½ **teaspoon baking powder**
½ **cup toasted walnuts**

Preheat oven to 325°F. Butter an 8 × 8-inch baking pan.

Cream the sugar and butter together with a mixer until light and fluffy, about 5 minutes. Melt the chocolate and add eggs, vanilla, and the sugar-butter mixture. Mix 2 to 3 minutes. Sift together flour and baking powder. Gradually add flour to chocolate mixture, stopping the mixer to scrape down the bowl several times. Fold in walnuts by hand.

Pour batter into prepared pan and bake for 30 minutes or until a toothpick inserted in the center comes out clean.

Cool completely in pan on rack. When cool, cut in squares. Serves 6.

Chocolate Fudge Puddle Pudding
Almost too good to share

Uncooked, this pudding looks like a disaster, but heat transforms it from a milky mess to a rich sponge. Vary with different or no nuts, dried fruits, and amount of coffee essence.

1 stick melted butter
2 large eggs, beaten
2 tablespoons coffee essence
1 pint (2 cups) whole milk
1¼ cups soft dark brown sugar
¾ cup self-rising flour, sifted
⅓ cup cocoa butter
¾ cup walnuts
Golden syrup to taste
3 tablespoons whiskey, brandy, or rum

Preheat oven to 325°F. Mix the butter, eggs, coffee essence, and ½ cup of the milk. Add 1 cup of the sugar, plus the flour, cocoa butter, and walnuts, and stir well. Pour into a greased, 1½-quart ovenproof dish.

Heat the remaining milk to just below boiling point. Add the syrup, stir until melted, then add the alcohol.

Sprinkle the pudding with the remaining sugar, and pour over the hot milk mixture. Bake in the oven for an hour. The pudding should be springy to the touch with a rich pool of chocolate sauce underneath it. It's great with crème fraîche or whipped cream. Or try it with a spicy compote of dried figs or prunes.

Serves 8.

Profiteroles with Chocolate Sauce
Made for sharing

For cream puffs:
1 cup water
6 tablespoons unsalted butter, cut into pieces
Pinch of salt
1 tablespoon sugar
¾ cup all-purpose flour
4 large eggs

For chocolate sauce:
½ cup heavy cream
8 ounces quality chocolate
Ice cream of your choice

Heat oven to 400°F.

Profiteroles: Bring the water, butter, salt, and sugar to a boil in a large saucepan over high heat. Stir until butter melts. Add the flour and cook for about a minute. Transfer to bowl and add eggs, beating well. Transfer dough to a pastry bag, and pipe about 20 mounds onto a large baking sheet. Bake in upper part of oven for about 10 minutes. Reduce temperature to 300°F and bake until outside of puffs are crisp and golden, about 15 minutes. Transfer puffs onto baking sheet on a rack to cool.

Chocolate sauce: Heat the cream in a heavy-bottomed pot over low heat. Add the chocolate, melt, and stir together with the cream. Remove from heat and allow to cool before using.

Cut each cream puff in half horizontally. Fill the bottom half with a small scoop of ice cream. Cover with top half. Top with chocolate sauce.

Serves 10.

Chocolate Mousse
For adults only

This recipe relies on melted chocolate. To melt the chocolate, break the chocolate in small pieces and then put it in a heat-proof bowl and set it over a pan of simmering water (the bowl shouldn't touch the water). Heat gently until the chocolate is melted, stirring occasionally.

8 ounces dark chocolate, melted
1 tablespoon unsalted butter
3 tablespoons brandy
⅞ cup double cream
3 egg whites
2 tablespoons superfine granulated sugar

Mix together chocolate, butter, and brandy until smooth. Whip the double cream until it forms peaks.

In a separate bowl, whisk the egg whites until they form soft peaks; then whisk in the sugar until firm peaks form.

Fold the whipped cream into the melted chocolate mixture; then gently fold in the egg whites. Divide the mousse among six small dishes or shot glasses, and chill in the fridge for at least 1 hour until set. Serve with a little double cream.

Serves 6.

Chocolate Truffles
Perfect for giving and receiving

5 ounces dark chocolate
2 tablespoons unsalted butter
¼ cup confectioners' sugar
1 medium egg yolk
2 teaspoons rum, brandy, or whiskey
Powdered or flaked chocolate or ground walnuts

Melt the chocolate and butter together. Stir in sifted sugar, egg yolk, and alcohol. Chill in the fridge for a few hours until firm. Form into 12 balls. Roll each one in chocolate or nuts. Refrigerate before serving.

Makes 12.

Rich Chocolate Ice Cream
Delicious

2 eggs and 2 yolks
½ cup sugar
1¼ cups half-and-half
8 ounces quality chocolate, chopped
1¼ cups whipping cream
¼ cup dark rum

In a large bowl, combine eggs, yolks, and sugar. In a large saucepan, heat the half-and-half and chocolate gently until chocolate is melted. Stir well to blend; then bring to a boil, stirring constantly. Pour chocolate mixture into egg mixture, stirring well; then transfer to top of a double boiler or a bowl set over a pan of boiling water. Cook, stirring well until the custard is thick enough to coat the back of the spoon. Strain into a bowl and cool. In a large bowl, whip the cream and rum until stiff, then fold into the cooled chocolate mixture. Pour into a rigid freezer-proof container. Cover, seal, and freeze for about 4 hours until firm. Scoop into chilled serving dishes.

Makes 6 to 8 servings.

Chocolate Waffles
Comfort on a plate

4 tablespoons butter
2 ounces high-quality chocolate
1½ cups all-purpose flour
1 tablespoon baking powder
1 tablespoon plus 2 teaspoons sugar
2 eggs, separated
1¼ cups milk
Melted butter

Melt 4 tablespoons butter and chocolate; cool.

Sift flour and baking powder into a large bowl. Stir in sugar. Make a well in center, add egg yolks, and mix thoroughly. Gradually add milk, alternating with chocolate and butter mixture. Beat thoroughly. In a bowl, whisk egg whites until stiff but not dry. Fold egg whites gently into chocolate batter. Brush a waffle iron with melted butter and set on medium heat. Pour on a small amount of batter and close waffle iron. Cook about 1 minute on each side or until both sides of the waffle are crisp and golden brown. Top with whipped cream, sprinkle with cinnamon, and serve with hot strawberries if desired.

Makes about 10 waffles.

Chocolate Fondue
Mmm

1 pineapple
1 mango
2 kiwis
1¼ cups strawberries
8 ounces seedless green grapes
2 or 3 dried figs
Fondue:
8 ounces high-quality chocolate, broken into pieces
⅔ cup whipping cream
2 tablespoons brandy or orange juice

Peel and core pineapple and cut into cubes. Peel mango and slice. Peel kiwis and cut into wedges. Cut figs into quarters. Arrange all fruits on six individual plates and chill. To prepare fondue, place chocolate and whipping cream in a fondue pot. Heat gently, stirring well until chocolate has melted. Stir in brandy or fruit juice, and beat until smooth. Place fondue pot over a burner to keep warm. Serve with fruit for dipping. In addition to fruit, you can serve with small cookies, sponge cakes, marshmallows, or meringues.

Makes 6 servings.

Chocolate Chip Cookies
Yummy!

¾ **cup butter**
¾ **cup light brown sugar**
¼ **cup dark brown sugar**
1 **egg**
1 **teaspoon vanilla**
1⅓ **cups all-purpose flour**
¾ **teaspoon baking soda**
6 **ounces high-quality chocolate**

Preheat oven to 375°F. Cream together the butter and sugar until light and fluffy. Beat in the egg and vanilla. Sift together, then stir the flour and baking soda into the butter mixture. Stir in the chocolate chopped into pieces. Spoon the dough onto a greased cookie sheet, and bake for 10 minutes.

Makes around 45 cookies.

Chocolate Mousse
Sensational!

6 ounces quality chocolate
1 pint heavy cream, well chilled
1 teaspoon almond extract

Melt the chocolate and let it cool for five minutes. Meanwhile, whip the cream and almond extract until very stiff. Gently fold the cooled chocolate into the whipped cream; you will see flecks of chocolate in the mixture. Spoon into six large wineglasses, and chill for 1 hour before serving.

Serves 6.

Chocolate Sponge Cake
Wicked but wonderful!

⅔ cup sifted cake flour
⅓ cup cocoa powder
1¼ cups sugar
6 large eggs, separated
1 teaspoon cream of tartar
Pinch of salt
1 teaspoon vanilla extract

Preheat oven to 300°F. In a small bowl, whisk together the flour, cocoa, and ¾ cup of the sugar.

In a large bowl, using an electric mixer, beat the egg whites, cream of tartar, and salt on a low speed until frothy. Add the remaining sugar. Increase the speed to medium, and beat until whites form stiff glossy peaks, about 2 minutes.

In another large bowl, beat the egg yolks and vanilla at low speed until blended; then increase the speed and beat until thick and pale in color, about 2 minutes. Pour the mixture over the whipped whites and fold until blended in. Sprinkle in the dry ingredients, folding in each addition before adding more. Gently spoon the batter into an ungreased 9 × 3-inch spring-form pan. Smooth and level the surface, and remove any air pockets. Bake the cake for about 45 minutes; then raise the temperature to 325°F and bake until a cake tester inserted into the center comes out clean, about 15 minutes more. Remove and allow to cool on a rack. Wonderful accompanied by strawberries and whipped cream.

Serves 10.

Chocolate Muffins
Perfect!

2¼ cups all-purpose flour
1 tablespoon baking powder
Pinch of salt

1 tablespoon plus 2 teaspoons sugar
2 ounces quality chocolate, broken in pieces
4 tablespoons butter, melted and cooled
1 egg, beaten
1 cup milk

Preheat oven to 400°F. Thoroughly grease a deep, 12-cup muffin pan or line with paper baking cups.

Sift flour, baking powder, and salt into a large bowl. Stir in sugar and chocolate pieces. In a small bowl, mix cooked butter, egg, and milk. Pour into dry ingredients and stir until flour is just moistened but looks lumpy. Spoon mixture into prepared cups. Bake in preheated oven for 15 to 20 minutes until well risen and golden brown. Cool in cups for 5 minutes before serving.

Makes 12.

Hot Chocolate
The ultimate pleasure prescription
Ready in 5 minutes

4 ounces high-quality dark chocolate
2 cups milk

The best hot chocolate is made by placing 4 ounces of high-quality dark or milk chocolate into a small saucepan. Add around 2 cups of hot milk, stir well to combine, and heat gently until it comes to a simmer. Pour into two large mugs, and top with a spoonful of crème fraîche and a sprinkling of grated chocolate, or top with miniature marshmallows.

Serves 2.

Hot White Chocolate

4 ounces white chocolate
4 tablespoons brandy or rum
¼ teaspoon vanilla extract
1 pint milk

Place the chocolate, brandy, and vanilla in a heatproof bowl inside a pan of boiling water. Place over a medium heat until the chocolate is melted. Remove from the heat. Meanwhile, place milk in a small pan over a medium heat until it boils. Immediately remove from the heat and slowly pour over the melted chocolate, stirring well. Pour into mugs and serve.

Serves 2.

Mexican Hot Chocolate

3.5 ounces plain chocolate
1 pint milk
1 tablespoon vanilla sugar
½ teaspoon powdered cinnamon
Sugar to taste
Pinch of chili powder (optional)

Heat the chocolate, milk, vanilla, cinnamon, sugar, and chili powder in a saucepan. As the chocolate starts to dissolve, mix well. Bring to the boil, then simmer. Whisk the mixture by hand. Serve when foamy.

Serves 2.

Quick Chocolate Treats

Are you hungry for chocolate cookies but the cupboard is bare?

* Brighten up plain biscuits by melting some chocolate over them.
* Peel a banana and put it in the freezer for 30 minutes. Melt some chocolate, and then pour over the frozen banana. The chocolate will freeze immediately. Eat right away.
* Create a creamy milkshake by breaking up a chocolate bar and putting it in the freezer for 15 minutes. Then, put the frozen chocolate in a blender with 1¼ pints vanilla ice cream and ¼ cup milk. Blend for 1 minute, and pour it into a glass.
* A mouth-watering chocolate fondue: All you need is 8 ounces plain chocolate and 6 tablespoons cream. Melt the chocolate in a bowl over a pan on hot water, stir until smooth, and whisk in the cream. Pour into small bowls and serve with fresh fruits and nuts.

* Make a chocolate sauce using 2 teaspoons cornstarch, 8 tablespoons cocoa, 1 pint cold water, 8 teaspoons sugar, and 2 teaspoons vanilla extract. Combine the cornstarch and the cocoa. Whisk into cold water in a saucepan. Cook, stirring often, until the mixture boils. Turn down the heat and stir until the mixture thickens; then add the sugar and vanilla. Store in a jar in the fridge for up to six weeks

* Melt some chocolate over a pan of hot water and spread inside a cut croissant. Leave it to cool and set; then heat your croissant in the oven for a breakfast or snacktime treat. Do take care when melting chocolate, because it scorches easily if overheated and will develop hard, grainy lumps. It will melt more easily if broken into small pieces. Do not stir the chocolate until heated, and even then stir it very gently. Stir when completely melted to make a very smooth mixture.